From OREOS *to* OLIOS

Sandra Brian Lore

PublishAmerica
Baltimore

Hardcover 978-1-4560-4974-4
Softcover 978-1-4560-4973-7
PUBLISHED BY PUBLISHAMERICA, LLLP
www.publishamerica.com
Baltimore

Printed in the United States of America

Dedicated to my family

For Mary Ann & Bob –
This will cure insomnia –
Sandy

From
OREOS
to
OLIOS

A glimpse of life from a middle class, small town kid in the mid-20th century, later propelled by marriage into the bigger world of the Foreign Service and what happened thereafter, so far...

Introduction

Although the word *olio* has been in use since about 1643, according to the Merriam-Webster dictionary, it was tossed into my vocabulary in the autumn of 2010. The first time I heard the word, in my mind's eye, I spelled it 'oleo' like that fake butter, but it has nothing to do with bogus butter.

Olio is a different entity entirely. My brother Mike introduced me to this olio which has many various meanings. Some synonyms are mixture, hodgepodge or a miscellaneous collection—as of literary or musical selections. Others are agglomerate, alphabet soup, assortment, clutter, collage, jumble, medley, mélange, mishmash, mixed bag, montage, patchwork, potpourri, ragbag or smorgasbord. Take your pick. I'm sticking with plain old *olio*.

What's in a name? This one was discovered when Mike and his wife Karen took us to the Thin Air Theatre Company's production of 'The Werewolves of Poverty Gulch' in Cripple Creek, Colorado. This melodrama (with high-spirited audience participation) was followed by a Halloween *olio*. They clued us in on what *olio* meant, because they had learned its meaning through a previous production by this troupe.

It was splendid. Exuberant people filled the stage in various costumes singing and dancing and acting silly. It was a hodgepodge to be sure. It was almost more enjoyable than the featured attraction due to the enormous talent and improvisation oozing from the stage.

The melodrama had already provided excellent entertainment, and the actors were geared up and wired for even more ridiculous performances with their *olio*. To be sure, they were a talented group of young artists, singers and dancers. One-third of them had been trained in Virginia. Yet, we had to leave Virginia for Colorado to learn about them. Why hadn't we been involved with *olios* before now? I'd been living one all these years!

Due to the all-encompassing mixture of meanings for the word, I have named the collection of stories I've written From Oreos to Olios. I've made a decision to write only *olios* from now on. It will entail much less effort than sticking to a subject and joining paragraphs in a purposeful way. I can jump around and mix it up and call it what it is! Imagine that my stream-of-consciousness writing fits into an old description of mixed-up stuff in use since the 1600s. As my mother-in-law used to say, "It couldn't be better."

'They' say you must get hooked on a book in eight to twenty seconds. Mark, my husband of many decades, suggested I start with, "He held her close and ripped her bodice."

Hooked? Good. Read on. You'll never know whether or not there are more ripped bodices unless you do.

Always the professor, Mark recommended I say things with as few words as possible. I require many words to say anything, but I have omitted some adverbs. If you spot an adverb you don't like, would you just cross it out or ignore it? If there are too many words to read, feel free to skip some of them. Some chapters are short. Skip the ones you don't like much.

Writing about growing up in Middle America in the 1950s, my life could very well be typical of others' stories of that era. It was a good time to be a white kid in northern Illinois. I cannot speak for all my contemporaries who lived elsewhere under different circumstances.

I hope some of these stories will resonate with you. Ellen Kort, a former poet laureate of Wisconsin, said we all experience similar things in life. We know how it feels to be loved and to love. We know the pain death gives us when loved ones die. We know joy and sorrow, and we're all familiar with the holy mundane of everyday living. There are similarities in our journeys. In this way and many others, we are connected.

Thanks to friends, family and writing group buddies for their love and encouragement in this undertaking. Without them, I wouldn't have written this book. Good friends have read through it and made their considered comments. I am grateful for their 'attagirls' and support.

Pat O'Boyle facilitated our writing group. Without her, none of us in our 'pen pal' group endeavor would have pursued writing to the extent we have. We all appreciated Pat's kind suggestions made with love.

Murphy Henry educated me on everything I know about playing bluegrass fiddle music. She edited parts of this book.

Ethel Doherty, a fellow Foreign Service wife and delightful human being whom I met after retirement, edited the whole manuscript. If you meet up with either Murphy or Ethel, please tell them how thankful you are for their cuts. You'll never know how many unnecessary words got the ax. Good friends Ruth Hopkinson and Mary Louise Roth read through parts of the book and made helpful comments. My brother Mike read the original manuscript and offered great encouragement.

You may find some universal truths here and perhaps some shared experiences. You may recognize some attributes or foibles which exist in your friends and families. Or, you may think I should have quit while I was ahead and kept my stream of consciousness to myself. Too late. Too bad. It's all here.

I dedicate this book to my family—Mark, my peripatetic, dear husband for almost a half century, to our two wonderful grown children, Chris and Camille, to Chris' wife Barb and their son, James, our grandson. I hope they won't be horrified about 'Mummer' telling family stories. Also, here's to all my far-flung families—kinfolk, adopted Foreign Service families and fabulous friends—you have enriched my life beyond measure.

In re-reading letters from over three decades, I appreciate how our family was able to stay psychologically connected even though we weren't living in close proximity to one another.

I wept at one of Mom's letters written when my brother Doug was in the Army and stationed in Alaska, and we were thousands of miles away in the other direction in Rio. She wrote she was writing letters that morning because she needed to talk with the people she loved, and that was the only choice available to her—to reach out through the written word.

Several men from Doug's base in Fairbanks already had been sent to Viet Nam, and some had never returned. He would not be able to take leave before going. She left it at that. Her heart was breaking. In the end she was one of the lucky mothers whose son wasn't deployed to Viet Nam, so he wasn't killed or maimed in the conflict in Southeast Asia. I think of all the heartbreak families have suffered in the past and are suffering today because of war. I am not sure it is ever justified, but that is a discussion for another time.

These hundreds of letters, while living overseas as well as the replies from home, kept us in touch long before email, cell phones and other modern technology were invented.

Since the best time of my life is right now being 'obligationless,' I've added some of my thoughts and activities in retirement which began in 1999 when we moved to Winchester, Virginia.

So, that's the story. Watch out for adverbs and torn bodices. We begin with one of my happiest first memories—my brother Doug's birth in Sterling, Illinois. We'll end here in Winchester, Virginia with *olios.*

Sandra Lore
Winchester, Virginia
2011

From OREOS *to* OLIOS

PART I

Growing Up

The horrendous winter storm of 1942 is my first memory. War waged around the world, but in my corner of the planet, my brother Douglas Arthur was to arrive soon after the northern Illinois winds stopped howling. Although upstairs bedrooms were unheated, I remember that sleeping felt heaven-like because of the fluffy duck-down featherbed which kept my three-year-old body cozy and warm. The hot brick from Grandma Brian's oven placed near my feet made for a soothing, warm experience. I had no trouble sleeping while Mother Nature blustered outside my grandparents' old Victorian house.

Unusual in September, that particular snowfall in northern Illinois covered the earth with a clean white blanket just in time for my first brother's birth. I stayed with Grandma and Grandpa Brian in their big old white, wooden house, located on a large in-town lot where Grandpa's veterinary practice took up the east side of the property.

I learned many years later that the house was on the road to the Sterling Public Library, and Mom made many trips to the library as a high school student, but it seems not all the trips were necessary—she needed an excuse to walk past the front porch of Dad's house to see him and to hear his fiddling. Once after a spat, Dad played, "The Song has ended, but the Melody lingers on." I find that very romantic.

Old newspaper articles tell me that watermelon parties for the townspeople were held on the lawn in the summers before I was born.

Wonder why they stopped them? I love watermelon!

Speaking of food, I remember that Grandma Brian always called me 'Honey.' At dinner one time when I was a bit older, she asked, "Honey, would you like some rice?"

My response was, "I don't know." The bowl was filled with what looked like snow and duck feathers! Having never eaten rice, I didn't know if I wanted any, and Grandma didn't urge me to try it. She just passed the rice on over to Grandpa. After that, I never had to be asked to try things. Obviously, they enjoyed what they were eating. I wouldn't miss out on something new again until many years later when I was offered squid floating in its own black ink.

Doug entered the scene exactly 99 years after our great grandfather Frederick Brian was born. Frederick was the son of our German immigrant ancestor, Johann Jacob Brian.

My grandparents and I were at our house on the Freeport Road to welcome Mom and Doug when they arrived. Mom and Dad had bought five little acres to raise goats and kids. It turned out that Doug made a whole lot more noise than my baby dolls. Years later, I learned that because Mom couldn't stop eating delicious pears, and because she breast fed him, Doug cried more than most newborns. They both suffered from indigestion.

Since I had been so good during this visit waiting for Doug's arrival—I learned to blow my nose and to whistle—I was rewarded with a stuffed toy calico cat. Doug was named, but the cat was always referred to as 'the Calico Cat.'

Mom stopped eating pears, and Doug grew up into a remarkably wonderful playmate. Mom and Dad always said they were glad their first-born was a girl, because our playing together involved sedentary kinds of activities rather than boisterous boy behaviors. Doug went along with whatever I wanted to do and mostly followed my lead in play and games until he discovered baseball. 'Keep the peace' seemed to be his mantra.

Doug and I were great buddies all during our childhood. We didn't have lots of toys, but our imaginations made up for the lack of material goods. He was an outwardly happy-go-lucky person all his life. Even as a kid, he had more friends than anybody has a right to have. He avoided unpleasantness at all costs. "Skip it," was his response when he was met with opposition or some kind of misunderstanding. Those two words entered his vocabulary early in his childhood.

We were best buddies up until the day I was married when I acquired my new best friend. As young adults, we had season tickets to Chicago Black Hawks hockey games while my soon-to-be husband was doing an Army tour in Thule, Greenland.

Our shared experiences from childhood are sacred to me now. Doug died suddenly from a heart attack at age 64. He told me after our dad's six-month stint deteriorating in a nursing home that he wanted to die the way our Uncle Jake did—quickly from a heart attack. That's what happened. I will always miss him. The Calico Cat and I are still here.

Onto the American Dream

We moved from Sterling to Lidice, a suburb of Joliet, when I was in kindergarten. We were a long way from our extended family and friends. I don't have any recollection of the people who lived on the other side of our Lidice red brick duplex, but I remember the house and the back yard piled high with massive, smooth rocks. Off in the distance was the maximum security state penitentiary called Stateville, so solid it is still there. On one occasion, they say a neighbor came face to face with an escaped convict while she was hanging out clothes to dry. After that Doug and I always looked to our left and right to see if we could find more prisoners who got away. How could a secure prison allow inmates to walk out? Perhaps this was a ploy to keep us kids close to home.

From our bedroom upstairs, I heard Santa arrive one Christmas Eve. I never did see him, but I figured we were lucky he found our house out in the middle of nowhere. The chilliest Canadian clipper winds blew across the Illinois plain straight at us. We had left our home in Sterling for a new home in Joliet, because Dad had found a job.

It was from here as a first and second grader, I walked to the Cheney Elementary School—even in the snow and sleet. Sometimes neighbors with cars would drive us to school—what a luxury! Doug was too small to attend school, so he and Steffie the dog stayed home. Life was simple, placid, and Mom even might have admitted, dull.

16

Eventually Mom and Dad made new friends and stopped traveling back to Sterling to visit families and friends each weekend. My parents had been part of the Sterling community since they had both transferred to Sterling High School as juniors. Now, they were 100 miles away, on their own in search of that American dream after World War II. Riding across northern Illinois to and from in the unheated Terraplane car was always an adventure.

Our subdivision had been called Stern Park, but it was Lidice by the time we arrived. It was named after the Czechoslovakian village which was attacked on June 10, 1942, by the Nazis in reprisal for the assassination of a Nazi leader named Reinhard Heydrich. All men and boys over the age of 16 in the village were murdered while the women were made to watch. The women and smaller children were dispersed from the village and sent to concentration camps. Homes and buildings were razed.

Thousands of miles from this horrific scene, a group of citizens newly ensconced in this community re-named it Lidice in honor of the inhabitants of that destroyed Czech village. Hitler had vowed to wipe Lidice off the world map. To ensure his not being able to do this, Stern Park, along with dozens of towns around the world, was re-named Lidice just to be sure the name would be kept on maps forever.

Many years later, I learned about Mom's activism during that time. Rummaging through boxes of archives, I found the newspaper articles about Mom's being invited to Lidice, Czechoslovakia. Evidently, she was involved in planning of the annual remembrance of the horrific massacre. She also helped raise money for a memorial to the women and children of that small village.

I didn't know a thing about the Holocaust. I guess Doug and I were oblivious to it because we were too young to read the papers. Radio didn't include non-stop talk shows. Some of what I remember from that period is: lots of snow, playing Clara—the Clara who slept and dreamt—in the Cheney School production of *The Nutcracker Suite*, my dog Steffie and the weekly ritual of attending the Ottawa Street Methodist Church in the heart of downtown Joliet.

Being asked to share my penny bubble gum with Doug and Mom

is still a vivid memory. I always started chewing it first. Then, of course, it was too late to share. I still can taste that beautiful blob of sickening sweet pink which began as a rubbery rectangle and with considerable chomping transformed itself into a juicy, slippery delight which often drooled out of my mouth. Pennies weren't so easy to come by, so bubble gum was a rare treat. I wonder if it still is sold in pink rectangles.

Speaking of sweet things, Dad always liked chocolate. It does taste better than bubble gum. I'll bet if I had been asked what Dad loved more than anything else in the world, as a little kid, I would have answered 'chocolate.' (Later on, I might have said 'cigars.') Less than a week before he died in 1992, he asked his grandson David to buy him a chocolate bar from a vending machine in the nursing home.

Thinking about chocolate, while washing dishes recently, I recalled that when Mom and Dad entertained, their friends often brought boxes of chocolate candy to the dinner parties. Today, we arrive with wine of some kind, but my folks and their friends weren't drinkers, so the offering was candy—which may cost more than wine these days.

Doug and I always went to bed before the evening was over for the adults, but it just struck me that two pieces of chocolate candy remained in the box each and every time Mom and Dad had a dinner party. It was just enough for Doug and me, and it was never that awful jellied stuff. We always went searching through the 'empty' box the next morning, tearing through the little paper cups, and we always, always found two pieces left for us! What a nice gesture—especially since Dad was addicted to the stuff. This behavior began when we lived in Lidice when Mom and Dad began reaching out and inviting new friends into our home.

Just Stuff

Our family had a penchant for small stuff. A glass amber frog is one of the small objects in our house. It is a 'found' object—lost for some months where it had been stored in a safe place in my grandmother's pine needle sewing basket where I had stored other special small belongings from my childhood. This frog has been in my safekeeping since I was eight or nine. It was given to me when I was home from school in bed with either measles or chicken pox—both common childhood diseases when I was growing up. Seems we kids had measles of one kind or another every year.

On the Internet from Kids Health for Parents I learned there were thousands of cases of the measles in 1950, but in 2002 there were just 44. Most of the time, the cases occur where there are lots of kids, some of whom haven't gotten vaccinated or whose immunity has diminished.

The bedroom was darkened so my eyes would not be exposed to light. Mom delivered the lunch tray one day holding the frog which had belonged to my dad's grandmother. It would join my collection of little things. There must be something wrong with someone who goes through her entire life thinking a thumb-sized glass amber frog is special. I wonder if he came from one of the famous West Virginia glass factories, or was he a cereal box or Cracker Jack prize. The company began including a prize in every box in 1912 (the same year Dad was born). We'll never know its origins. I have 'googled' fake frogs but haven't learned a thing.

A frog (or even a toad!) would have cheered up any child of my generation sick in bed with measles or chickenpox. This frog is precious to me for the memories it holds for a simpler time, a simpler childhood, a simpler life. Imagine! A tiny thumb-sized amphibian has stuck around for more than 60 years, sometimes hiding in my grandmother's tiny pine needle basket. It must be true—that this little symbol brings good luck in many cultures—ours included.

My 11ᵗʰ Birthday Present

My Dear Sandy:
Your birth-day present is going to be something different this year.
I am giving you Mattie. If you keep her and love her as many years as
I have then you can pass her on to your grand-daughter, and she will
still be here to make some little girl happy. I would suggest that you
not un-dress her as her little body is frail and broken. You see she is
way past fifty years old.

Maybe you would like to hear the story of how Mattie became my
doll. When I was a little girl I lived in the country. My playmates were
pet chickens, cats, a dog and several dolls. One day my sister and her
husband who lived about ten miles from our place came to visit us. On
the way they found a little duck that had evidently gotten lost from the
other ducks; they caught it and brought it on to me. I was delighted to
get it and at once gave it the name of Kimmie. Well, he grew up to be
a beautiful green headed drake with feathers of various colors.

My mother had other ducks and when I was in the house Kimmie
stayed with them but the instant I went outside he would come to me.
I spent many happy hours with him for I would go hide and he would
hunt until he found me and if I was out of sight where he couldn't see
me he would stand near by and make the funny little noise that drakes
make when they try to talk.

When I was eight years old our large two story house on the farm
burned to the ground. My father had had it built just four years before.

After that we moved to town and of course Kimmie moved along with us. He had gotten older by that time and had developed a rather mean disposition for he tried to kill all the little ducks we were raising. You see in those days we could have chickens, ducks and most anything we cared to have in town without restrictions.

One day my mother said to me "Josie you have got to get rid of that duck or he will kill all the little ones". Well, without further delay I picked up Kimmie took him over to the poultry house which was about a block from where we lived. My heart was heavy as I carried him over there and on the way I kissed him thirteen times. (That part I would not remember if I hadn't heard my mother tell it so many times, for I told her when I got back home.)

I knew all the time what I was going to do with the money I got for Kimmie. He brought 75 cents. I had feasted my eyes many times on the pretty dolls in one of the stores, in those days dolls were on display the year around and not just at Christmas time as they are now.

Well, I went to town at once, your Daddy will remember how close the old home place is to the main street in Belle Plaine. With the 75 cents I purchased Mattie. I spent many happy hours with her in my child-hood days but she never quite took the place of Kimmie. I think a pet with life is more precious than any other kind.

Well, honey this has turned out to be quite lengthy, and maybe all I have written won't interest you at all. I hope your birth-day will be a happy one. Wish we could spend it with you. You are growing to be a bigger girl each year and must be a lot of pleasure to your mother and daddy.

Write to us,
With Lots of Love,
Grandma

I did love my antique dolls as much as my contemporary ones even though I couldn't play with them and change their clothes. Even as I child, I found them to be perfectly beautiful. Mattie's sweet porcelain face is surrounded by cascading golden curls tied up in velvet ribbons. Dressed in chiffon, her embellished dress is decorated with tiny white beads, and champagne colored embroidery and velvet ribbons surround her waist. Her cloth feet sport hand-sewn boots of real leather and her white cotton underwear is trimmed in lace (should you want to know that much). Like all ladies of her time, she holds little purse on her arm which is fraying. There is a feather sewn onto her butterscotch colored felt hat just under the silk button flowers. Of course, Mattie can't replace a lively duck, so I see why Grandma might have preferred her mean-spirited old drake to Mattie who kept—and continues to keep—a silent vigil.

My doll Marie came from my mother's Aunt Marie. Mom wasn't allowed to play with this doll when she was young, but it was willed to me. This doll has dark auburn hair and blue eyes which are a perfect contrast to her creamy pink colored satin dress embellished with netted grey lace roses. She too has leather shoes and fancy under frocks. People did take care of these lovely creatures. Note that Grandma Brian admonished me not to undress Mattie because she was fragile. That is how people preserved these dolls for posterity. (Hmmm, I must be posterity! Did you ever look at yourselves that way?) It doesn't look like Aunt Marie changed her doll's clothes either.

Mattie and Marie watch us ascend and descend the stairway between the first and second floors of our house from a special cupboard purchased in a Pennsylvania flea market almost 20 years ago. Other precious 'stuff' is housed in this cupboard also—like the shriveled up sixth finger I was born with on my left hand. By the way it looks like a dead fly. Of course, the amber frog is there too!

I know Grandma would be happy to know that Mattie would continue to be part of the family and would be cherished for even longer than Grandma probably imagined. I'll bet my mother would have taken care of Marie had she been allowed to touch her as a child. These two dolls are part of the 'stuff' I cherish. I hope they will be passed on through several generations more—even without a granddaughter. Maybe nieces will treasure them. Maybe our grandson, James, will have daughters.

Swearing In

I spent more time with dolls than with profanity, but I'd like to tell you about my first 'bad' word. How innocent was life then! We were living in our second house in Joliet. First, we lived in Lidice. The silica gel plant where Dad sold advertising closed down. His next job with an advertising agency didn't last too long because one of the two partners committed suicide.

Then, we moved to Vine Street, closer to downtown Joliet. Dad found a job selling radios and new-fangled, small black and white TVs at the West Side Radio Store just a few blocks from our house. Perhaps that's the reason we had moved to that location. Dad could walk to work. Maybe the Terraplane quit running. His next and last position was with Prairie Farmer and came with a company car. Good thinking!

So here we are in the late 1940s—Mom, Dad, Doug and me— living in a typical brick bungalow of the day. The house was square and brick, and one entered the living room from the front screened porch. It boasted two typical dormer windows on the top floor—an easy mark of a bungalow. Wooden columns separated the dining room from the living room with the kitchen at the back of the house. On the right side of the dining room, you entered a small hall with Mom and Dad's room off to the right and Doug's and mine to the left with a bathroom in between.

The basement had a cistern for catching rain water although it was

24

no longer in use. It also housed Dad's big old barn loom where he began his weaving avocation. My dollhouse, which Dad had made for me, was in the basement, too, set up on a card table. It was electrified and painted barn red with two floors. A Christmas tree bulb served as a light in each room. I thought it was the finest thing a kid could ever have. I don't know whatever happened to it although I still have the early plastic and wooden furniture which graced each room. A washing machine and clothes line for inclement weather were also in the cellar.

The other part of the house which I considered remarkable at the time was the attic. Mom and Dad made it into a dorm room for Doug and me. As you came up the stairs from our former bedroom, you were greeted by our crystal radio set (made with Dad's help) which sat at the top of the steps. Our twin beds were lined up side by side on the long wall topped by designer quilts of primary colors made by our great Aunt Alice.

Doug's quilt was big Ds pieced together and quilted, and mine was made of big Ss which I still have. I don't think we ever liked the dormer room as much as the other bedroom. Now, I can see why it was a necessity—grandparents and old family friends who visited needed a place to sleep, so a third bedroom was constructed in available space.

The garage and a large yard with big garden were at the back of the house. Both hold fond memories. The garage was a theater at times—but more on our 15 minutes of fame later. The garden probably produced great stuff, although I didn't appreciate it very much as a kid.

As a child, I officiated at many pet funerals and wondered about separate heavens for the various species. Would there be separate heavens for Protestants and Catholics since they had separate churches here on earth?

Most of our friends went to Catholic schools, so my brother and I knew how to say the 'Hail Mary' when called upon to do so. We liked the Catholic kids' shorter version of the Lord's Prayer. Although some kids had learned the 'debts' version instead of 'trespasses,' we all got along. We were ecumenical and didn't know it. None of us was particularly sophisticated about our religious training, but we were all careful not to step on the other fellow's toes. It is obvious all our parents were interested in us kids learning their takes on religion.

Life was slow-paced. We conducted funerals for any dead thing we might come upon. The dead birds and smallest animals were buried in my dad's old King Edward cigar boxes strewn with flowers—hollyhocks, dandelions and other blooming things we'd find around the yard. If in a few thousand years archeologists dig in that back yard, they may wonder about the significance of burying goldfish, turtles, cats, dogs and birds in the same spot and—those which would fit—in cigar boxes.

The fad in those days was to go to our friends' houses and yell out their names in our biggest voices. It seems so primitive to me now. The Smith kids were three favorite friends, and we'd cross the alley and call out, "Oh, MaryAnn," or "Oh, Pat," or "Oh, Jimmy" with all the lung power we could muster. Either a kid would come out or a parent would yell out that they were eating dinner or not at home or whatever. Today, the neighbors not to mention the parents would undoubtedly deem that noise pollution. We kids were always yelling for somebody now that I think back on this impolite behavior. Yes, we could hear kids yelling for someone other than us once in awhile.

We had one famous person on our street, slightly older than we—Georgiana was her name. She lived up the block on the way to the neighborhood grocery store (where I often dropped glass bottles full of milk on my way home). She married one of Bing Crosby's sons in an underwater ceremony off the coast of Florida. I always thought it would be beyond 'cool' to have a crooner father-in-law.

Now, let's return to that bad word—so mild by today's standards. You know which word I mean, so I won't type it out. I don't use the word. When a word is too overused (as the F word is), it loses its punch and becomes nothing more than a verbal tic. My father-in-law had mastered the art of using exactly the right cuss word at exactly the right time. He used these words judiciously. He's the only person in the whole world who ever called me a 'GD intellectual.' Bless his heart.

So, there we were in the kitchen, Mom and I, washing and drying dishes. I don't think Doug got into that act until we moved to Plainfield, and he was considered old enough to take on dish washing and drying responsibilities. We alternated nights then—which meant Mom was always on duty.

So, I asked, "Mom, what does f - - - mean?" She was blown away by the question. Mom always kept her cool, but from her demeanor, I thought immediately I should not have asked. Momentarily, she regained her composure and asked that we finish the dishes first and then we'd talk about it. I suppose if I'd been smart, I would have asked my friends the meaning and then verified it with Mom. Or, I would have found out and left Mom out of the discussion.

I did keep quiet till the dishes were done. I realized she was coming up with an answer to my question. After dishes were dried and put away, we sat ourselves down at the kitchen table, and she proceeded to tell me about the birds and the bees. In those terms. "Birds do it, bees do it!" Heck, she could have written those lyrics for Cole Porter.

The most important lesson was that the word wasn't one we should use. Additionally, I learned about seeds being planted by the male species in a special place where babies grow—right under their mothers' hearts. That was soft, sweet and sustained me for years. It was pointed out that that F word was a very foul way to talk about the closest of human relationships. It demeaned them. I think she was right.

So, there you have it—my initial introduction to the power of language. It is indeed a powerful tool. How else would I have remembered after all these years what my first 'bad' word had been? It is so mild compared to today's speech. Times have changed.

The Honest Kid

Thomas Jefferson once said, "Honesty is the first chapter of the book of wisdom."

Decades ago, at nine years of age, I reported one crime and committed two. One day my classmate Jack lavished me with glittering rings and beads from his married sister's jewelry box. (I won't give you his last name. He's probably an Illinois politician or some such these days). Proudly, I scurried home after school to show Mom how nice Jack had been. What was I thinking?

"Sandy, Jack has no business giving you 'gifts' which belong to his sister. You must take these jewels to the principal." So, I carefully carried the baubles back to Miss Bolton. Mom made me honest.

Miss Bolton was almost gleeful hauling Jack into her office. I stood still watching him squirm. It was a terrible time—one of the boys actually 'liked' me, and I had turned him in. The jewels were just a cover for the principal's real agenda.

She started the dialogue, "Now, Jack, I know you're almost a man, being a fourth grader and all."

Jack grinned sheepishly.

"What's the brand? Camels? Lucky Strikes?"

Grinning stopped. He turned ashen and looked rather unmanly. He had been seen smoking near the playground fence—a much greater offense than swiping his sister's diamonds and pearls.

While he was scolded, I diverted my thoughts to other jewelry—

the dime store kind other girls were wearing. When Miss Bolton finished dealing with Jack, the smoking jewel thief, I told her I was missing my necklace. Would she mind if I checked the lost and found box? Smiling sweetly, she told me to go right ahead.

It took only a moment. "I found it!" I squealed. On the heap of assorted lost caps and mittens was a necklace of large translucent pink pearls. I would have preferred white, but pink would do.

"Sandra, this must be your lucky day!" Yeah, right! I couldn't wear the darn thing—it wasn't mine, and the rightful owner might spot it. No showing my honest Mom. I was a lousy thief. As no great ideas surfaced, I returned the necklace to the box after hiding it overnight in my desk. I told Miss Bolton it wasn't mine after all—the clasp was different.

My best friend Judy sat behind me in class. Stumped in a geography quiz that same year, I carefully turned around and whispered, "How to you spell the answer to #11?"

"E-G-Y-P-T"

Burning hot and shaking uncontrollably, I couldn't handle being dishonest. There would be no more stolen property for me, and if I didn't know an answer, I wasn't going to ask how to spell it. I was going to be honest—and wise.

These 'crimes' plagued me for many years, and I never stole or cheated after fourth grade! It just felt too uncomfortable. I wonder if Jack learned the lesson too, or did he spend his life behind bars.

Stepping Out

About this same time, as a fifth grader, I received my own invitation to a party. I had been invited to a friend's home during the December holidays. Dale's words were, "Sandy, my family and I would like you to come to our house for some of my mom's home-baked Christmas cookies." I had never met a cookie I didn't like. I surely wouldn't turn down this kind of invitation.

Dale, who lived on the other side of the Cunningham Elementary School, was my boyfriend from third through sixth grade. I could easily walk from my house to his for this special party. A foot shorter than I, his very blond hair was always cut the in the 'in' style of the era, a cool crew cut.

My thought was to devour cookies, because my little brother Doug wouldn't be there grabbing more than his share. Mom must have considered it a tea party (the traditional meaning of tea party) kind of affair because I wore my Sunday best.

Dale, his older sister Connie and his parents were present at the party. Entering their living room felt warm, cozy and very welcoming with a fire blazing in the fireplace. The Christmas tree in all its glory was lit up on the far end of the room. Someone took my coat, and I was asked to have a seat. Presently, Mrs. Kramer entered the living room carrying an enormous round silver platter just covered with the most beautifully decorated, scrumptious looking cookies you can imagine.

Mrs. Kramer smiling said, "Sandra, please have some cookies."

And that's when I took the platter, set it on my lap and started eating cookies as fast as my little mouth could chew them and my stomach could digest them. I didn't hear anyone say, "Pass the platter please." It was a great party. Now, there's a happy childhood memory! Someone removed the platter and rescued me from my *faux pas*, but I don't remember that part of the afternoon. Anyhow, I was probably already full of cookies so didn't mind sharing at that point.

Another equally important holiday rolled around soon after Christmas—Valentine's Day. I was probably still on Cloud Nine from the previous February where Dale was concerned. He played an integral part in my always having a Happy Valentine's Day. He had an unparalleled talent for making elaborate, large cardboard Valentines. I was the recipient of these works of art several years running. Had I had enough sense to save them, today they would be considered museum quality artifacts from the fifties.

The valentine production began each year after Christmas. Valentines were foot high pieces of cardboard, painted in the right shade of red with straight-from-the-heart-written-especially-for-you poetry. In my childish eyes, it was great verse. I remember only part of one poem from the period, "I play a flute. That makes me cute." I was the only recipient of these Valentine gems (so far as I knew).

Happy memories of Dale include my first 'date.' Dad drove us to downtown Joliet to see "Harvey." He picked us up after the movie. No hand holding. No first kiss. No popcorn. We were probably sixth graders. Why in the world would I think this was significant enough to write about, eh? Well, he was the first boyfriend. I will not write about any of the others. Nobody ever topped Dale's Valentines anyhow.

The Unmet Friend

During our time in Joliet, a meaningful event in my life revolved around a little girl named Janice Sheraton whom I never met. Janice never realized the lessons she taught us kids. The Sanders girls took dancing lessons with her, and they learned Janice had a fatal disease. This was our first encounter with the possible death of a kid like us. We felt we had to do something to help.

After we were informed about the illness of this girl, we heard her parents didn't have the money they needed to treat her kidney disease. The diagnosis was nephrosis. None of us knew what that meant, but we did know it was very serious.

A newspaper article from the front page of the *Joliet Herald News* tells the whole story (August 18, 1948). We neighborhood kids decided to 'have a show.' Since one pays admission to a 'show,' that's how we figured we could make some money to help Janice with her medical condition. We charged just a nickel, but some paid more since it was for a good cause. Our pals came back for each showing and always paid admission again.

We got our garage cleaned up, installed a hanging curtain and went to work on our numbers. The two dancing Sanders girls wore golden tap shoes. Is that not the epitome of having 'arrived' as a kid? They're also pretty cute—with natural curly red hair. Mary Ann held a lollipop and sang and danced to the 'Good Ship Lollipop' not looking a thing like Shirley Temple. Georgiana was Dorothy from the Wizard of Oz.

Sharon wore a nifty leopard outfit and used our dog Anitra as a lion or tiger. The boys collected the money and took care of the gate.

I got some quick tap dancing lessons, and I can still do the step: jump, shuffle, ball, change. Well, I don't know if I can do the step. I know how it's supposed to go.

So there we are—saving humanity at an early age. We didn't make enough money on the show, so we scavenged the neighborhood going door to door asking people for more. We went way out of our comfort zone to streets where we knew no one. And, as I recall, nobody turned us away. We felt empowered. We had done something to help another child. We engaged the audience to help with the canvass for additional revenue.

I hope I'll never forget the event. Now, I have no one to talk with about it. Doug and I used to giggle over our *chutzpa* putting on a SHOW! This effort on behalf of another child was one of the high points of our childhood. And, I got to sing and dance.

So, this is another tale of long ago and far away and making something from nothing and doing unto others as you would have them do unto you when life was a whole lot simpler for nine-year-olds and their friends.

Janice didn't live. Many people helped to extend her life by assisting in defraying the cost of medicines she needed. I would hope that kids might do this today. Probably their parents would write checks instead—and for more money. Janice made an impact on all our lives, and most of us didn't even know her. In her illness she taught a handful of kids to be concerned about others. She never knew the lesson she taught us.

Whatcha Got There?

It was summer time. We didn't have television. Our parents must have been searching for activities for us. Five of us little neighborhood kids labored on a nearby truck farm for a very short while. The work ended soon after this conversation.

The mean-spirited bully man asked, "Whatcha got there?"

"Two-hundred eighty five bundles," I replied.

He screamed, "You cheatin'. Can't count good."

At the age of 10, I protested, "Count them yourself. There are 285 bundles."

My brother was only six and a half. We were all little kids. This incident has stuck in my craw all these years. I chew on stuff. I've been masticating for almost six decades about this.

Joliet, Illinois, 1949. Some truck farmers wanted help getting stuff ready for market. Did our parents see a 'help wanted' notice and sign us up? They couldn't afford to send us to camp.

Bushel baskets of thousands of unpeeled, dirt encrusted scallions were dumped at our feet. We peeled off the outer skin to make the scallion clean for the market. We tied them together, 24 to a bundle. That was a penny's worth. We kept good count and stacked the onions into custom-made cardboard boxes.

The big old boss man scoffed, spit and repeated, to me, "You cheat."

At that moment, Mr. Smith, our ride home, showed up. We five dirty, hot little kids piled into the car and left, unpaid.

We didn't get the $2.85 owed to us on our last day. We had 285 bundles of 24 scallions each or 6,840 onions or 1,368 per kid if we peeled at the same rate. We evidently had no recourse. That number 285 has stuck with me all these years.

The 'cheat' was hiring little kids. That was illegal even in 1949. He paid way below the 40 cents/hour minimum wage. We returned home stinking of onions, and Mom and dad talked about 'ethics' at dinner. I believe this guy was the first dishonest adult I met.

This is a small, insignificant story from the last century—peeling onions for a two-bit truck farmer.

Now, move into the 21st century. Inhumanity is rampant where work ethics are concerned. Think about the injustices in our own communities done by us to other ethnic groups—namely those people without documentation—those 'illegal' immigrants who are being cheated at every turn. They're 'illegal' just like we were as kid laborers in 1949. We weren't feeding destitute families. We were making money to buy bubble gum and baseball cards.

"So, whatcha got there?" Whatcha got is some 37 million undocumented people in the US today—some working under the table for low wages often cheated by people looking to make a faster buck. Who's the culprit? The employer? The employee? I believe that answer is simple. Think of all the stuff stuck in craws today.

"So, whatcha got there?" Whatcha got is a serious moral dilemma which needs to be addressed before another half century goes by. In 1949 we see middle class kids with white privilege screwed. Today, much harsher penalties await 'undocumented' human beings who share our planet who are here now working to alleviate dire poverty. They are being cheated. So, whatcha gonna do?

Fiddling

And, then, I began fiddling around. I heard every word Mrs. Feeney said that day, "Class, I am pleased to announce again this year, our violin teacher Mr. Herath will be giving group lessons after school to fourth graders."

Wow! I could hardly contain myself. I tore the two blocks home as fast as my little legs would carry me to tell Mom and Dad about this development. I already had my own violin. Dad had a few. I just knew one of them would work. I was absolutely certain Mom and Dad would sign me up.

I had been born with six fingers on my left hand. My brothers always thought I should have joined a circus. I guess the protrusion didn't resemble or feel like a finger as it had no bone. Bone or not, that's when Dad rushed out to buy me my first violin—a quarter-sized instrument—but still too big for a baby.

The doctors concurred, "The extra finger must come off!" Just think, with lots of practice and a sixth finger on my left hand, I might have been a great fiddler today. As there was no bone in the finger, the doctor just tied a string around it tightly, and it fell off in a couple of days. I still have it. It resembles a dried up, dead fly under glass. Maybe it belongs in a museum. However, it's housed in the same cupboard as the amber frog.

The group lessons lasted about a month, and I was off to the Joliet Musical College on Chicago Street by bus for private Saturday morning lessons. The bus took me to Joliet's bus station within a block of my destination, a three-story building right next door to a Greek restaurant. I climbed three flights of steps to the musical college. One time I knew the number of steps, but that has now receded way, way back in my memory. The Joliet Musical College was the only establishment emblazoned with black letters on the glass front door of the building.

I must tell you an aside. At the second floor, there was another glass door which read, 'Universalist Church.' I remember asking Dad one time when on our way to a recital, "Dad, what kind of church is that?"

"That's a church full of strange people, Sandy. Don't pay any attention to them." (And now I am one—a Unitarian-Universalist).

Most people took piano lessons. Also at the Joliet Musical College were a few voice teachers—'has-beens' from the Chicago opera. Mine, Miss Lucille, smoked the whole lesson long while I coughed and choked and sang away. I did that for awhile in high school. Mostly, however, I went there weekly to learn to play the violin—or to discuss politics—which I enjoyed more.

Mr. Herath's studio was behind his wife's desk, and one could reach it from the incoming hall—not from the main reception room. In fact, there were two rooms—the smaller one was always free for practice while one waited. I didn't ever feel the need for that. Lessons were to be a half hour in length, but I was always there an hour. So was everybody else. We all got our money's worth and then some.

Mr. Herath liked to pick on me because I was a Democrat. My parents taught me I was a Democrat from an early age. I started violin lessons about the same time as Mr. Truman was elected—that was the year I got to stay up all night and tally votes along with the radio announcers. I always loved Mr. Herath who reminded me of my Grandpa Brian—also a Republican of the same vintage.

Back to fiddling. I could tell how I was doing with each lesson. If Mr. Herath found favor with you from one week to the next, your picture was included on his enormous bulletin board of students. When he was feeling less kindly toward you, it wasn't there the following week. Almost before even greeting Mr. Herath, I'd take a sneak peak at the bulletin board to see if my photo was thumb-tacked onto it. Sometimes I saw it there but certainly not every week.

Lennie, a pipsqueak who started playing years after I did, always had his picture prominently displayed. He grew up, majored in music, finished college and he and his new bride took over the musical college after the Heraths' retirement. I heard from several sources later that they thought it was too labor intensive and found another line of work rather quickly. When the instruments and equipment were sold at auction, Mom and Dad purchased a souvenir for me—a piano stool with crystal balls held by paws.

Back to Mr. Herath. "Sandra, I would like for you to play each note as if it were a pearl."

A pearl? I never heard a pearl make a noise. In fact, I didn't even know any pearls—just those fancy beads called 'faux pearls.' There it is—the reason I never played well—I never knew how a pearl should sound.

Through high school, I played the violin. As a 7th grader, we moved ten miles away from Joliet to Plainfield. I was the only person in the whole town who played a stringed instrument. That wasn't easy. Everybody else was in band. They marched in parades. They entered state contests every year and brought home blue ribbons. The kids told me I played worse than Jack Benny.

With the move, the bus trip became longer and more expensive. At some point during high school, the fee for the lesson was increased from 75 cents to a dollar an hour. Mrs. Herath who was the office manager reluctantly informed my parents. Maybe if I had practiced more he wouldn't have had to increase the amount?

I can remember three times when I skipped lessons. In fact, I only did it when I was within walking distance from home—when we still lived in Joliet. The Salvation Army needed my fiddle money. I recall two Christmas seasons where I gladly gave them every nickel in my pocket—including the nickel for the bus fare home. The exercise walking home probably did me good.

Sometimes when Dad was home, I called after my lesson so he

could come get me. On the other end, a man's voice answered 'Baxter and Jennings.' Of course I knew it was Dad. So he changed his phone answering service response to 'City Dump.' In any case, he'd drive the mile into town to pick me up to save the nickel bus fare. Gas cost about 23 cents a gallon in those days—and the gas stations gave you premiums like glasses and dishes to stave off the competition. I never asked him who Baxter and Jennings might be.

The really selfish spending—when the lesson money didn't go to the Salvation Army Santa—was to see the movie 'Red Shoes.' Daydreaming as a kid, I often imagined myself a ballet dancer. When I heard 'Red Shoes' was on at the Orpheum, I spent the lesson money and went to see it.

Not being too smart about this sneaky, extravagant behavior, I got into the theatre all right and saw about three quarters of the movie. I never learned the ending as I had to get home on time. My parents would have worried had I not returned home when expected.

Recently, I rented the DVD and saw the ending along with three friends who hadn't seen the movie in years. It seemed so stilted the second time around. We four silly girls lined ourselves up on the sofa like birds on a high wire, wore our red shoes, munched popcorn and giggled.

Dad used to remind me that it wasn't Massenet, Mozart, or Saint-Saens being judged. It was I! Of course, that still holds true. And, I do appreciate the great European geniuses of the past who left such incredible musical legacies for future generations. But, being too busy growing up, I never did them justice when playing their music—except in the middle of the orchestra where I could play away—hitting clunkers at times—but still as a part of the whole dramatic, dynamic process of producing beautiful music.

Everybody should have music in his/her life. Everybody! It serves as a vitamin pill for the soul when the soul may need it most. So there's the tale. Here's another: James, our little grandson, when a fourth grader, called me soon after school had started. With tremendous excitement in his voice, he chirped, "Grandma, I'm going to play the violin!"

I squealed, "Wow! A Fiddle! James! I'm thrilled!"

His excited tone changed to disgust as he corrected me on the proper name for the instrument. "Want to hear me play the violin?"

The plucked sounds of out-of-tune strings traveled over the phone lines from Maryland to Virginia. "You need tuning, "I offered.

"That's next week, Grandma. They'll tune it then, and next week, I'll play you something with the bow, because we're not supposed to touch it yet."

Next week came and went. No phone call. No bowed fiddle—whoops, violin.

I learned a few days later that his parents made him give it up before he had begun. He had too many other obligations, and his behavior needed some kind of modification. He'll be better at the trumpet—his first choice, he later told me—which he thought he would start in fifth grade. I'm for once grateful that I wasn't as smart as my little grandson. I fiddled away a chance to play well, but in doing so, I discovered a retirement hobby that is more exciting than anything else I can imagine. James may have quit too early. Then again, one day he might be an old retired guy with a trumpet.

In the Middle of It All

We moved to Plainfield in 1951. I thought my life was perfect until I stopped to think about both the good and bad. Located just a few miles from the very center of the US population in the 1950s, it was practically a perfect place for six years—my years in junior and senior high. They were bittersweet years. I felt like an outsider for many reasons. Our ancestors had not plowed the nearby fields, we were Democrats, I played a string instrument instead of a band instrument and I was a liberal even as a kid and didn't know a thing about racism.

But, wait a minute. Picture the perfect part: I had one brother, and then another when I was 17 and a senior in high school. Who would have thought that Mom and Dad were doing that in the bedroom next door to mine. Also, my brothers and I had two parents. And, we had various and sundry pets. Cats and dogs—Minnie Minoso, Handsome Ransom Joseph Jackson, Jr., and Anitra were some of the menagerie.

Life was simple and revolved around the village green, churches and school. Family, friends and fiddle played an important part in my life. Today Plainfield's corn fields are completely wiped out and are now covered with suburban sprawl. It's not a small town with 1,800 people any more. Now, there's no special delivery mail by Ike, the man with Downs' syndrome. Is there even special delivery mail any longer?

I played the violin but would have preferred to play the clarinet so I could take trips with the marching band. Almost everybody was

41

in the band. It was not easy being the only one in town playing the violin.

One day a classmate named Larry chased me home from school—a distance of two blocks. When he caught me he tried to break my little finger because he didn't like how I played the violin. Luckily, Dad was home when I got there. His solace was, "Sandy, the world is full of Larrys." Darn! That's not what I needed to hear, but at least I only met that one. He grew up, and we became friends.

Eighth grade graduation was a real milestone in my young life. I had a beautiful dress for that occasion—a frothy pale sky blue organza number. I turned to serenade the graduating class during the solo violin piece and played with my back to the audience. Is that why I received so much applause?

Then, as the band played "Pomp and Circumstance," I cried during the whole recessional and all the way out the door. I wasn't crying about the violin solo—I just didn't want to go to high school. Perhaps I've never been quite ready to grow up or move onto the next stage. I seemed to be happy right where I was. Maybe I was unstable. Hmmmm…

Being the lone Democrat wasn't easy either. There were a couple other Democrats in town—my parents were two of them.

My nickname was "Nig"—short for that horrible racial slur because I had invited Jesse Owens to a high school assembly to speak about his experiences with Hitler in the Olympics. At the time, he was living in Chicago and did come to our school to address the entire school about his experiences. When I returned for my 25th high school class reunion, one of my classmates, hollered across the gym, "Hi, there, Nig!" He used to be one of my favorites of our class of 51 souls.

As a freshman, I was the only girl in my class invited to the prom. I don't know why my parents let me go, because they were very strict about social engagements. My date was a senior, the only child of a prominent family. He was a nice young man and we had a great time at the prom because he was a fabulous dancer. I was rather 'puffed up' being the only freshman there. He committed suicide just days before he was to leave for college. By our sophomore year in high school, I wasn't the only girl in my class invited to the prom.

People made fun of one of the boys in our class, because he was never clean, and his hair was never combed. He left town before we ever got to high school, but since he walked home the same way I did, I tried to befriend him. I think he probably didn't have any running water in his house. I know his dad was in prison. How awful it must be to be a kid in such circumstances. I wonder what ever happened to him. After all these years, I've met so many people on the outside looking in.

Home was so safe and secure for me. Dad was on the road at least three nights during the week, so Mom had sole responsibility for us kids and running the household. She didn't drive but was so good at organization that food was purchased for the coming week each Saturday when Dad was home to take her to the grocery store.

I think we were clued into things running out when creamed eggs on toast was served for supper. We stretched turkey at our house. We'd have the bird for Thanksgiving. What was left would be frozen and made into some kind of casserole for Christmas. Come Easter, the fare was turkey soup with rice. Mom was a master at stretching food and making it taste delicious. Early childhood training and being a child of the Depression contributed to her culinary creativity. And, she now had a freezer to help her preserve food from one holiday to the next.

Since Dad was an amateur photographer, he spent many hours in the darkroom developing and printing pictures from his week on the road either selling advertising for Prairie Farmer or drumming up circulation for the paper. Mom ran the household, even when he was home, although he always had the last word because he was the man of the house. Sunday consisted of Sunday school and church, a big family dinner after church and sometimes a 'ride' around town in the afternoon when gas was cheap.

Mom worked at the meat packing plant in town for 75 cents an hour so I could buy dresses at Steiner's Dress Shop. Many clothes had come from my cousin Rita (who still weighs about 103 pounds dripping wet) or were sewn by Mom. I had a job at Owens restaurant, and when Mike was born, Mom stayed home, and I earned my own store-bought clothing money.

We had itinerant men walking the railroad tracks in those days. The Clarksons (owners of Owens Café) fed them at the restaurant. I'm sure that word was passed on from one vagrant to another. They'd sit in the back booth, and with my tip money, I'd always buy them a glass of milk and pie with ice cream. I thought those things were good for you. As a kid, I figured if I were homeless, that's what I'd like to eat.

My very best friend Sandy had polio in 7th grade. Every other house on our street was affected by polio. Several people died. Sandy had a bum leg from then on. She was such a good friend. I'm sorry we haven't kept in touch, but I guess after 50 years, most people tend to drift apart.

I'll never forget sitting in my 8th grade classroom across the street from the Evangelical United Brethren Church as Sandy's family emerged after her dad's funeral. He died rather suddenly when her mom was pregnant with her little sister Carol. I could weep when I think about it now. Sandy married and had two kids. A black cloud must have floated above her, because her husband died of a heart attack at 40.

So, family, friends and fiddle figured prominently in my childhood home of Plainfield. The best part is that I had a loving family—I always wanted to please my mom and dad and never knowingly caused them any trouble.

A Developing Groupie

I was allowed to stay up all night to hear the election returns. I had been taunted for many weeks by my classmates with "Dewey's in the White House winding up the clock; Truman's in the garbage can eating up the slop." The year was 1948. My mom and dad were planting that 'democratic' seed.

We tallied the returns from the big, old Phillips radio which sat next to the piano just inside the living room of our brick bungalow. After the huge upset, I went off to school the next day bleary eyed but ecstatic to announce to my class that in fact Truman had won the election. I'll never forget the tone in my teacher's voice when she said, "We'll have no more talk of politics in this classroom, Sandra." So much for civics lessons.

After moving from one sophisticated Illinois town (Joliet) to another (Plainfield), I became a great admirer of Adlai E. Stevenson, our Illinois governor, who had been nominated by the Democratic Party to be its standard bearer in the 1952 and 1956 elections. My bedroom in our big old white frame house faced Lockport Street, and I filled the three floor-to-ceiling windows with gigantic colored posters of him.

It didn't take long for my male classmates to paint "I like Ike" on the sidewalk and to dump manure on the front porch. (Farm kids knew where to get manure—lots of it). Those were the days of poodle skirts. I had a skirt which I wore often and proudly with 'Madly for

45

Adlai' in block felt letters sewn across it. I even had my picture taken with the chairman of the Democratic Party (Stephen Mitchell) while wearing it. Unfortunately, it didn't start a trend.

By the election of 1956 I was still the lone Democrat in school but had earned some respect in the little town. Debates at school always had a number of Republicans participating, and I always took the Democratic side by myself. Because of my opposition on all fronts, 'plucky' was the praise from the Speaker of the Illinois House of Representatives, Warren Wood, himself a Republican who lived in Plainfield. I often invited Warren Wood to forums at school. We debated things like Universal Military Training and whether or not Hawaii and Alaska should become states. I'm still passionate about politics.

Margaret

This story is a special part of my childhood. Looking back on it, I think every kid should either collect stamps or correspond with a pen pal in another country.

With the diagnosis of rheumatic fever, Margaret was ordered by her doctor to stay home from school for a whole year. Four-thousand miles away in Plainfield, Dorothy came to our 7th grade class one day with her name and address—Margaret Trushell from Paisley, Renfrewshire, Scotland. Margaret was anxious to have an American pen pal. I quickly raised my hand. I thought it would be fun to have a Scottish pen pal. Thus begins this tale.

Only a century ago, forty-seven years was the life expectancy for men and women in our country. For almost a half century—or a total lifetime for people 100 years ago—letters between Margaret and me flew across the ocean—weekly for the first few years, less frequently while I attended college and more or less semi-annually once we were full grown married adults with family responsibilities. The letters always began 'Dear pen pal.' We were great friends as teenagers—sisters across the pond. She had a younger sister, and I would have two younger brothers after 1956, but ours was a special kind of 'safe' sisterhood—we shared secrets and they were secure with both of us.

As young 'teeny-boppers,' (if a teenager in the 50s could be referred to as a teeny-bopper), we poured out our hearts to one another about the significant events in our lives—boyfriends, of course, growing pains, parents' expectations, school work, lost loves and whatever else we deemed important to share. Her letters came in the form of an 'air gram' a flimsy sheet of light blue paper, the kind of paper carbon copies were made from, which folded into an envelope and flew more cheaply than regular letters and envelopes. Margaret's air grams came with the stamp of the Queen already imprinted on them. As no enclosures were allowed, important events in our lives were duly photographed and sent off to one another in regular envelopes requiring more postage.

Paisley, Renfrewshire, Scotland may have been a small place— just a dot on the world map—but Plainfield, Illinois, was insignificant entirely. To counteract the boredom which the town's name implied— plain field—we had many dances in the school gym. To help pay for all these ball gowns, I worked in Owens Café beginning at age 15, and as I've told you, I made enough money in tips to not only help to feed the daily stream of hobos from the railroad tracks but also to buy clothes at Steiners' Dress Shop. As I grew in teenage sophistication, I knew I needed off-the-rack clothing to succeed in life.

We were so 'old timey' that daily recreation after wolfing down lunches in high school was jitterbugging to World War II music in the big hall outside our locker rooms.

Thus, with every dance, I wore a new fancy, frilly frock. With every dance, Dad took my picture on the ornately carved walnut staircase in our home. With every dance, Margaret received a photo. I was sharing my life with her. Did I have a tin ear? What I learned on meeting Margaret was that she viewed me as a rich American girl. Our correspondence began not too long after World War II when life was difficult in Britain. Shortages I'd never dreamed of were commonplace in Margaret's life. Read the book, *84, Charing Cross Road*, if you haven't. You'll get some idea of the extremely difficult life Brits endured after the War—well into the 1950s.

When Margaret finished high school, she married John, and I went on to college. It happened that while I was in college, my mom and dad went on an all-expenses-paid grand tour of Europe as chaperones for some 100 retired Midwestern farmers and their wives. As Dad was the circulation director for the three farm publications who sponsored the event, he was evidently just the right age to be assuming this responsibility along with a couple of strong women—Mom and the female tour director. Although the average age of the tour group was somewhere in the 80s, there were only two heart attacks during their six-weeks of travel, and nobody died.

A highlight of their trip, beyond Rome's ancient forum, the leaning tower of Pisa, and Europe's other greatest hits, was meeting Margaret and John who came aboard their ship while they were docked someplace in Scotland. It was a thrill for all four of them.

They met again a few years later when Mom and Dad returned to the British Isles. By that time, Margaret had two boys—Kenneth and Brian—and to help make ends meet, she washed babies' diapers in her kitchen sink for the neighborhood moms. My dad immediately gave them a check and suggested a practical use for it—they could buy a washing machine with the money, which would ease Margaret's workload. Both my Mom and Dad were thrifty, so imagine their surprise on learning that Margaret and John spent that $100 on dinner and dancing New Year's Eve.

As my parents were not dancers, I'm sure they never did understand that mentality. Dad was a very generous man and continued sending them $100 each Christmas for many years. Margaret and John danced—year after year. The last pictures I have of Margaret are from a video of their youngest son Graeme's wedding, which took place when we were living in Brasilia in the mid 90s.

Margaret and John's fabulous ballroom dancing was videotaped at the reception. Every movement they made was together in lockstep. They had been perfecting this effortless-looking skill of gliding around the dance floor for many decades. A classical ballet itself could not have been more beautiful. Life had always been difficult for them. Their escape mechanism was dancing. It could have been booze or drugs, but instead their frustrations, trials and tribulations melted away as they waltzed, fox trotted or boogied across dance floors.

On that glorious day in 1976 when we met, we had lunch with them at their home and ate dinner at the hotel where our family stayed that night. The hotel was the one where they danced on New Year's Eve. This was the trip to Great Britain when the kids got their adorable puppy, a sweet but stupid Cairn terrier from Nottingham. We named him Geordie McVitie—Geordie because we had passed a pub named the 'Jolly Geordie Pub' and thought that was perfect for our new puppy. We also all became very fond of McVitie digestive biscuits during that trip, hence we added McVitie for his second name. Dogs need two names, don't they? I'll write about our pets over the years later.

On that trip, we also discovered scones, clotted cream and Scottish strawberry jam. I may never get over that taste delight and remember asking Margaret if she knew how to make scones. She gave me her well-worn recipe book, the kind you're given by the manufacturer, and I've treasured it ever since. While she searched for her recipe book, she opened several cupboards in the kitchen. Only one had any food in it—a can of peas. I shudder to think how much sacrifice went into our special lamb salad lunch that day.

Margaret's mother told us that Scotland was at its best for our visit. She allowed as how they didn't always have glorious, sunny weather like what we were experiencing. Golden yellow 'broom' covered the hillsides in all directions.

We were accustomed to quaint English accents because we were living in Brussels at the time where many Brits also lived. Feelings of pride in our English language facility ended when we met John, Margaret's husband. In order to find him, we had pre-arranged a meeting place at Glasgow's airport. We met John in the airport waiting room near a car which was going to be given away to a lucky person with the winning lottery ticket. We were, of course, more easily identifiable than John was. John opened his mouth and out came a mouthful of unintelligible syllables. He spoke Gaelic! Margaret never told me that. So, hers and their kids' job during our time together was to translate his contributions to the conversations. In any case, we were driving our old blue Peugeot, which John loved. He wished he had such a car to tool around in. Their family lived in council housing and never had a car.

We found common ground rather quickly even with the language barrier. He kept teasing me that he was going to fix me haggis— stuffed sheep's stomach. I thought that was probably not edible food, but now that I've eaten it several times, I'll have to admit it's edible but bland. We left the Hunter family cherishing many memories of our time together. We always planned to meet again one day, but it never happened.

Margaret's photographs as a young girl showed her to be a clone of Ann Blyth, a Hollywood beauty of my generation. Years later, Margaret's letters talked about her delightful grand daughters. I decided she should have all the photos and letters I had saved over the years. I didn't have all of them, unfortunately, but I could never have imagined how thrilled she was to receive the hundreds of letters and dozens of photographs Mom or I had saved over the decades. She re-read the letters and began sharing her childhood with her young grand daughters. No gift could have made her happier.

We had just returned from a two-year assignment in Newport, Rhode Island, in the summer of 1997 to our home in Vienna, Virginia, when a forwarded letter arrived. Margaret had mailed the letter to our Newport address which was forwarded to Vienna. She wrote that she had inoperable lung cancer. She said she wanted to say goodbye to me—her American sister. She wrote me about how meaningful our long friendship had been to her. With heavy heart, I answered her letter. I hoped it would arrive before her death. I knew she had only a short time to live as she was under hospice care when she wrote me. Another era was about to end, but I was very grateful she was so thoughtful and wrote to say goodbye. Would that we could all write goodbye letters to loved ones.

Graeme wrote me after her death that she had indeed received and read my letter the day before she died. Only a handful of relationships in my life have lasted as long as my friendship with the little girl who suffered from rheumatic fever. For over four decades, air grams arrived in our mailboxes—no matter where in the world we were living. I still catch myself at times leafing through the day's mail hoping for some news—to find a light blue air gram from my dear pen pal. I will miss her always.

Mr. Larson, My Mentor

Outside the family circle, Arthur J. Larson was the biggest influence on my young life. No one who ever knew him would forget a man of his stature. He and his family were friends of ours. More important, he was my Sunday school teacher for several years. Inspired by the Character Research Project (CRP) of Union College in Schenectady, New York, he and Dad helped Dr. Ernest Ligon with his CRP research. Based rather loosely on the Beatitudes, I spent years having my personality molded by Mom and Dad, Mr. and Mrs. Larson, the Department of Psychology at Union College and as well as several others interspersed here and there.

Mr. Larson was an engineer and worked for Commonwealth Edison all his life. We always thought he was a Republican—one of those moderate ones hardly in existence these days. My dad never could understand why Mr. Larson, who looked at the world exactly as he (Dad) did, voted Republican. I later learned from his daughter Marcia that he was a registered Democrat—one of the few in DuPage County. I wish he and Dad had gotten that straightened out before they both died. Men sometimes don't talk as much as they should.

Because Mr. Larson gave so much of his income to charity, he was audited each year by the Internal Revenue Service (IRS). He was the most generous human being I've known personally—a real humanitarian. Marcia told me, "I think he delighted in lugging all of his materials into Chicago on the Burlington so he could have this conversation with the IRS annually."

The beginning of my awareness of lack of civil rights and unequal social justice happened during Mr. Larson's watch. My introduction to the Marshall Plan and what we might do to help Japan after Nagasaki and Hiroshima also happened during his tenure as my teacher. He and another Sunday school teacher took several of us for aptitude testing to the Character Research Project headquarters in Schenectady, NY, when I was an 8th grader. All the other kids were high school age, so I was closely monitored.

In addition to the tests, I learned it is a long drive from northern Illinois to Schenectady, NY. When not being tested, we visited a chewing gum factory (where we were given samples) and a glove factory (where no samples were given out).

I remember a few parts of the testing. One question which I'll never forget was, "I like my mother, but _____." I had to finish the sentence! My response was, "she takes all her pies to the church."

Another part was to name the woman I most admired in the world. I couldn't decide between two people. I named Eleanor Roosevelt and Sally Hamilton. I just couldn't choose one over the other. Sally Hamilton was a classmate of mine, her mom made her fabulous princess-seamed dresses, and she danced on top of the bass drum at football games.

While Sally danced on drums, our Sunday school class was involved in big picture pursuits. We put out a newsletter. My solution for Japan and its unimaginable problems after the war was simple. I think now it wasn't all that unreasonable. I suggested that all other countries of the world send them seeds for food. That way nature could step in once again and feed their population. I'm somewhat taken aback at the big problems we small kids were being introduced to during those years.

Lynchings were still taking place in the south. Although not a daily occurrence as far as we knew, they were not rare events. I got my bottom spanked by a policeman at Lookout Mountain in Tennessee when our family was there on a vacation. I didn't know the difference between the white and 'colored' water fountains—both clearly marked. So I tried the colored one. The policeman, while hitting me on the bottom, told me in no uncertain terms, "Little girl, you drink from the white fountain. Can't you read?" It didn't help my understanding. The water tasted the same.

Dr. Martin Luther King was already a hero in Mr. Larson's eyes. I don't think a Sunday went by but that we didn't talk about race relations. The whole business just seemed ludicrous to me. It still does. We've come a long way since then. We've a long way to go. I finally met Dr. King at a sociology forum at Illinois Wesleyan University when I was in school there. Unfortunately, because of all our moves, I've lost the book he signed for me. It was about the measure of a man—the brotherhood of man and the fatherhood of God.

In the early 80s, Mr. and Mrs. Larson visited us in northern Virginia while on a bus trip from their retirement home. I worked hard on the dinner menu, because I knew I was feeding both a gourmet cook and a gourmet eater. The only part of it I remember now is the chocolate mousse cheese cake dessert. It was a special visit—they could see my little family and how we lived decades after our first meeting them. Mrs. Larson had given Chris a baby shower in Naperville, and now Chris and Camille were already in elementary school.

The Larsons had retired to the Uplands Retirement Village in Pleasant Valley, Tennessee. Although I never visited them there, I always thought it was the perfect place for these two fine human beings to enjoy their last years—what name could top Pleasant Valley? As Mr. Larson never met a mechanical or electrical problem he couldn't fix, he was very useful to the fledgling retirement village when it came to problems they encountered. I know Mrs. Larson played bridge. They both loved their time there, and it was perfect for them until Mr. Larson had to go into the nursing home. He died when we were living in Portugal, and on receiving the news from Mom, I cried like a baby. I sat in the winter garden room of our ancient house and wrote a letter to Mrs. Larson.

She wrote back that she wished so much I had shared my feelings with him while he was alive. He never realized the impact he had on his Sunday school charges. I just thought he always knew the force for good he had been. He and my dad were the only philanthropists I knew personally.

We all meet wonderful characters during our lifetimes. Each is unique. Art and Madge Larson were two of the most unforgettable characters I've ever known, and I will always feel blessed that they were part of my life. I was just one of the many beneficiaries of their examples for living a good life. Marcia got it right when she once told me our two families were mutual admiration societies. We felt the Larsons were the personification of good people living truly Christian lives. This is often a rarity among self-described Christians.

The Mighty Pen Pals' Exercise

My writing group—we call ourselves Pen Pals—were asked by our facilitator Pat O'Boyle to write about something we love or value. There are so many things to consider. My value tale begins with Mrs. Vinson and ends with Ibuprofen.

She was an elderly woman with beautiful snow white curly hair, who lived across the street from us. Mom visited Mrs. Vinson almost daily even though she had a full-time caretaker. This seemingly sprightly looking woman, paralyzed with arthritis, was bedridden. Her daily exercise—which we found fascinating—was wiggling the fingers of her hands, one by one, as she counted to 100 and back again in German. Although she was able to talk and to smile, only her fingers still moved. When I think about this aged, sweet lady, with sparkling eyes, I'm caught up short realizing that she was probably only slightly older than I am now. She suffered from debilitating arthritis.

Her cream-colored wooden house with an unused front porch, embroidered with Victorian gingerbread, was charming. Her bedroom was at the front of the house. From there with her bed facing a large window toward Lockport Street, she could see lots of kids and a few passing cars.

Of course, at this time in my life, only a few families could boast of owning a television set. Mrs. Vinson had a radio I recall—just like my grandparents—but she didn't listen to baseball games like my grandpa did. I'm not sure what she could find interesting on the radio—perhaps her escape mechanism included soap operas.

Another kind of radio, WILL, a public broadcasting station out of the University of Illinois at Champaign-Urbana began its 'educational' broadcasting in 1941 but had a very weak signal and a small listening audience. I remember my dad's excitement at its becoming a stronger presence ten years later with a larger radius than 100 miles. He now could listen to classical music all over the state when he traveled.

I guess because of Dad's love of music, I just always assumed Mrs. Vinson appreciated fine music. Her hair, which rivaled the 18th century composers' wigs, her facility with German and her *joie de vivre* (which I do not know how to say in German) portended this love of classical music of composers such as Mozart, Beethoven, Schubert and Hayden. Although I don't know with certainty that she heard beautiful music from her radio, it makes her plight less arduous somehow to think that her pain might have been somewhat alleviated by music.

Mrs. Vinson was the extreme example of what could happen to a person with arthritis. My mother also had arthritis, but as she was a generation younger than Mrs. Vinson, Mom in her 70s and 80s was able to have two hip replacements and a knee replacement. The latter was so painful that she told Karen, her daughter-in-law, not to let her do that again. In the end I believe she would have been happier with two artificial knees.

In writing about something I really love and/or value, I've spent hours, days and weeks trying to come up with a suitable 'one thing.' I have too many choices! It would take volumes to write about all I love and value. My lovable something turns out to be a necessary something just like Dad's music which kept him humming. Ibuprofen. My gears are oiled, greased and rotating when necessary right after breakfast every day. I wish Mrs. Vinson also had had the benefit of my miracle drug.

That's what I'm grateful for, that's what I value so much—Ibuprofen and a practically pain-free life. Mrs. Vinson and others before her didn't benefit from the many things we take for granted. Painful arthritis has some trouble squeezing itself into my busy life, because I'm fiddling it away with fingers that mostly work. Now to attend to the brain and memory. Wonder what medicine I can find for that? I'll bet the best idea may be Mrs. Vinson's—wiggling fingers and counting to 100 and back in German. I can wiggle fingers. Who will help me to get started with the German?

Oreos!

Here is where the oreos fit into the story. When I became a teenager and learned to dunk, Mom had gone to work outside the home. Maybe I had some inkling about dunking before then, but I can't be sure. Plainfield was a very small town. Mom didn't have the complicated life which working mothers have today. She, my brother and I returned from work and school at about the same time each day. Everybody in our village had a two or three block walk from anyplace else in town.

The ostensible reason for her going off to work was so I could wear fancy frocks from Steiners' Dress Shop, the only dress shop in town, and the most exclusive one in all of Will County as I recall. Mom was a wonderful seamstress although I'm not sure she really enjoyed the activity. My little brother Doug had several special Easter jackets made by her when he was a little boy. By the time my littlest brother arrived, Dad was making enough money for store-bought clothes for the whole family.

The meat patty packing plant where Mom worked bought cookies wholesale in huge cardboard containers. I don't know how much they weighed, but their cylindrical size was at least 15 inches high and 12 inches in diameter. They held a whole lot of Oreo cookies. In any case, the employees were allowed, and perhaps encouraged, to buy Oreos in bulk. With mom's working, she didn't have as much time for baking, so this must have been the beginning of the modern era and the 'value added product,' i.e. cookies ready made.

My brother Doug and I tore home after school just to get some dunking done before Mom arrived 15 minutes later. We perfected the art, and let me tell you, there is nothing quite as grand as dunking Oreos in a cold glass of milk. Your mouth and chin hang over the glass so you don't dribble. The art consists of holding onto the very rim of the cookie—clearly stamped around its edge. Then, without getting your fingers milky, you dip that Oreo into the milk, leaving it no more than two seconds to saturate the biscuit. Pop it all into your mouth at once. Before you've swallowed it, dip the next cookie. Repeat. Do this as many times as you can in whatever time allotted you—if you don't want to get caught in the act. Don't worry right now about the drips. Just keep the drips returning to the glass of milk where they originated.

These beautiful slurping memories surfaced this week when I actually bought a package of Oreos. I surreptitiously ate them—only six at a time or so—and tonight there are only a handful left.

"Where are the cookies?" asked Mark. "I haven't tried one yet."

He's got to be quicker on the draw than that. After all these years, he should be more aware of the Oreos disappearing act.

Mark proceeded to tell me, "It was wrong to eat all those cookies". 'Wrong?'

Now that I've spent so many decades perfecting the art of slurp dunking, I don't want to quit—just because it might be 'wrong.' Maybe I'll just lay off the Oreos—when Mark's watching. Ah! Oreos: dunk, dribble, down, repeat. Go for it!

CRP's PS

With Mom and Dad involved with the Character Research Project at our church, my brother Doug and I spent some time 'practicing' asking the question, "What's your PS?" Today, when discussing most any subject in either of my brothers' families or mine, someone will ask that question.

It does not sound like a scintillating conversation asking, "What's your PS?" There's more. You've got one, too—a PS, that is.

Through the previously discussed Character Research Project (CRP), we kids in our Sunday school classes were presented with some new notions. Theories of character development were 'tested' throughout the country in various church denominations.

One of these notions was called 'perceived situation' or PS. Now you know. Yes, of course, you have one too!

In very different circumstances and at a very different time, the ideas embodied in this question helped to frame our family's code of ethics and to teach us how to live in community with others. I've decided to go public with its meaning.

Doug, Mike and I, along with dozens of other kids, were taught in speaking with others to inquire about their take on the subject. As we all look through different eyes, no one observes the same situation in exactly the same way. Therefore, in conversation, if we voice our 'perceived' situation, it's only fair that the other person's view is heard as well. Some of our political leaders might do well to consider this notion.

This avoids jumping to conclusions, a 'poor form of exercise,' my dad used to say. How simple! Ask the other person for his take on the situation.

Try it. Put yourself in a position where you aren't aware of the other person's opinion. Rather than goading him or her into something, dictating what you want from the person or ignoring his or her ideas completely, take it down to a simple, basic question. Ask, "What's your take? What is your perceived situation? How does it look from your perspective?" You may be surprised at what you learn.

From just two people discussing an event, a plan or an issue of any kind, one is able to learn another's viewpoint. Then, ideas might mesh, or grow, or mushroom, or snowball. Maybe even some world problems could be resolved by these simple means. Common ground might be discovered. I know that sounds grandiose. On the other hand, if we all did this, consensus might be reached more often. Who says even really big problems couldn't be solved in this way?

If we listened more to the other fellow's perspective, the result could lead to happier and more contented lives for all of us. Let's all start now. Pick a subject. Then ask someone else the question, "What's your PS?"

Enter Michael Edwin!

Drum roll please! An auspicious date in the family's history took place in Plainfield, Illinois on September 19, 1956. Here's what happened:

Although Doug and I didn't sit together at the high school assembly in the gym, we were both thinking about that baby who would be joining the family soon. What happened during the assembly has been forgotten. However, at the very end of the convocation, Mr. Reynolds, the guidance counselor, went to the microphone to make the following announcement, spoken in his usual droll manner, "Sandra and Douglas Brian need to see Mrs. Pennington at the school office at once." We knew why we were being called to the office. A baby was on its way. Mrs. Pennington told us we had a baby brother, and he and Mom were both doing fine. Dad had called the school soon after Mike was born and asked them to tell us about his arrival. We literally ran the two blocks home to lunch. That night, Dad reported that Dr. Duffy suggested Mike be started on 'steak and beer' having entered this world at the whopping weight of 10 ½ lbs!

It is not uncommon for a woman today to have her first child in her forties postponing children until after a career or at least till 'later.' This wasn't the norm in 1956, however. Our family consisted of Mom and Dad, me, the older kid, and brother, Doug. Here it was 14 years since Doug's birth, and our Mom was pregnant.

Our parents didn't tell us the situation for quite a while. Doug and

64

I didn't think our parents did 'that!' Years after the fact, I learned Dad had proposed the rhythm method (which the Catholics used successfully evidently). Mom got pregnant. For several months she starched his underwear to remind him how that rhythm method didn't work for them. However, both Mom and Dad often readily admitted Mike was the best thing that ever happened to them. He did keep them young—and on their toes. The date for delivery was set for September 19. A Caesarean section was in order because of Mom's age. Dr. Duffy knew it was going to be a big baby.

Mom's niece, Rita Nicholas Olson, just happened to have done her nurses training at Silver Cross Hospital in Joliet, so she assisted in the delivery and came to Plainfield and stayed with us for a number of days to make sure all went well.

That night, I was to cook chicken and mashed potatoes for Dad and Doug. I often helped with food preparation, and Mom and I had uproariously great times making up operas while doing dishes after dinner. (Dad's idea was to instill in me that operas were just ordinary peoples' lives set to beautiful music). Therefore, we felt washing and drying dishes fit into that ordinary category and sang opera, often! Sometimes we made up our own tunes. More often, we borrowed the tunes from a great operatic composer and changed the words to suit us. (We thought we were so clever! At least Mom had a clear lyric soprano voice).

Next to Mike's birth, the second most extraordinary thing happened that evening just as I was getting supper on the kitchen table. The phone rang. It was Mom. She had gotten up out of her hospital bed and walked down the hall to a pay phone to see if I had gotten the potatoes mashed. (Remember, a pay phone meant one put a nickel in the phone receptacle then dialed the number). In today's world, a half century later, a new mother would punch a number on a cell phone sitting next to her.

Mom and Dad celebrated their 25th wedding anniversary on February 2, 1957. Great Aunt Clara sent them a note stating that our great grandparents (Frederick and Margaret Almira Milligan Brian) also celebrated their 25th anniversary with a new baby in the house, our Grandpa Brian, who was born in 1890. I wonder if great grandmother starched great grandfather's underwear. I believe if she did, that family story would have been passed onto their progeny.

A Surprise Party

Mom and Dad were married on Groundhog Day in 1932. In 1957 as their 25th anniversary approached four months before my high school graduation, my 14-year-old brother Doug and I cooked up a surprise party for them. We knew this was a propitious occasion. We had baby brother Mike also, but as he was not even a half year old, we couldn't count on his help. Mom and Dad were an 'old married couple,' with three kids, 17, 14 and five months of age, and they were about to have their long-lived marriage celebrated.

My best friend Sandy lived on our street, so her help was enlisted. Her part in the scheme was to receive all the RSVPs at her home. Confiscating Mom and Dad's address book, I wrote out invitations to all the relatives. I knew they would be delighted to travel in the dead of winter to this big celebration. Bear in mind, to a 17-year-old, 25 years was a very long time to be married. They were married during the Depression and tried to work their way through college but ended up struggling to put food on the table. They dropped out of school and began testing their parenting skills on goats and the dear dog Steffie before ever starting their family seven years later.

Let's get back to the conspiracy. Mom got wind of the party plans, because a gift of silver from a well-to-do relative arrived at the house. She was rather taken aback at the prospect of 50 people coming to eat turkey and ham. She asked me how I planned to produce this food. Of course there was a plan. I figured Sandy's mom probably would be delighted to help, because I had no idea how to cook a ham or turkey. I think I also thought that the restaurant where I worked would probably be happy to help out, say with catering.

Back then, I had a part time job at the local café where tips were higher than the salary. I took piles of change to the bank to exchange for 25 silver dollars which were readily available in 1957. Doug and I hung them onto a three-dimensional plastic tree usually utilized for gumdrops at Christmas. We were pleased with our creation of silver tied up in netting on a white plastic tree.

The big day did arrive, although most people sent presents rather than risking accidents ice or snow-covered roads. (President Eisenhower's interstates had just begun construction). Nevertheless, Doug and I made lots of points on our plan to throw a party. Mom and Dad were quite bemused with our party organizing skills, or lack thereof. Our family didn't drink, dance or carouse around, so none of us knew much about the organization of any kind of big party. I think I thought it would be something like a wedding reception without a white dress.

Like many families' stories, I told and re-told this one over the years to Mark and the kids. In fact I told it to Chris and Camille just to point out that life was slower paced in those days; maybe kids were interested in pleasing their parents; and perhaps long marriages should be celebrated.

In 1989, thirty-two years later, Mark and I were about to celebrate our 25 years of marriage. We were home from our assignment in Portugal living in Vienna, Virginia. Camille had gone off to college and dropped out; Chris had gone off to college and returned to live at home for a semester to attend a local junior college. Remembering the stories I had told about his grandparents' 25th wedding anniversary, he announced that he would like to take us out to celebrate our anniversary. *"How kind!"* we thought. He invited Camille to come along.

On the appointed day, we waited for Camille, but she just didn't show up in time. We were all hungry, so the three of us headed out to the best Italian restaurant in McLean. Chris, on a poor boy's college budget, was making somewhat of a sacrifice in taking us to this nice restaurant. Although we were all disappointed that Camille hadn't gotten to participate, our moods were jovial when it came time to order. Chris suggested we share a large pizza with two toppings, because anything more than two cost additional money. So we did. And thus was given birth to another 25th anniversary story to dine out on for years.

When we're having pizza together these days, Chris' wife Barbara often tells us to feel free to order more than two toppings. She's already heard the story a dozen times. Camille did stop by and left a lovely, straight-from-the-heart gilded card for us on the dining room table. Since Barb and Chris have been married now for 16 years, James has a few years left to plan an occasion for them. Wonder if it will be pizza –maybe with a movie or extra toppings.

Ah! Events! Occasions! Milestones! They should all be kept simpler. Acknowledge the occasion and move right along because there will be another one before you know it.

Arranging Mom and Dad's anniversary party was both one of the first and one of the most joyful parties I have planned. Pizza with two toppings was one of the happiest I've attended. I love celebrations.

Growing Up a Girlie Girl

In our small high school of about 200 students, I belonged to all the organizations offered (for girls). Serving as editor of the school newspaper for two years turned me into a wannabe writer. Future Homemakers of America gave me my first stint at public speaking as a regional president. I remember two traumas in high school—learning how to do a somersault and catching on to shorthand. I was uninterested in sports. I was told I would get an F in physical education if I couldn't do a somersault. It took my parents' infinite patience and all the pillows in the house to make a soft landing for the lessons. Throw in lots of tears. Who needs somersaults anyhow? I passed that gym test and have never done another somersault.

In addition to those lessons, Mom and Dad helped me to figure out shorthand even though they didn't know a thing about it. I just didn't get it—writing squiggles on paper to represent sounds, syllables and language was a ludicrous idea. Until that point I had learned to spell words correctly. Now I was leaving out whole parts of words with these quirky little marks. They labored with me with as much vigor as they had mustered with the somersault lessons. I finally caught on to the magic. Once mastered, I considered going into court reporting but then reconsidered. Nobody does shorthand any more either. Somersaults and shorthand have their places, I suppose, but neither is important to me these days.

Mom always said I should learn to type so if anything happened to my husband, I could get a job. I typed fast—just about as fast as I took shorthand. These two skills have served me well over the years. I made money in college by attending lectures and taking verbatim notes, typing them up and selling them to the kids who didn't attend the classes. I also typed term papers—dozens of them—with at least two carbon copies. I imagine younger people reading this won't know what 'carbon copy' means. This all took place before copying machines (other than mimeographs) existed.

High school and college memories have receded way back in my memory these days. Once in awhile a reminiscence surfaces and I wonder what that old friend might be doing these days. I recently received the alumni magazine from Illinois Wesleyan University and learned that two former friends had passed away. It seems we were all just kids a few short years ago.

When I first arrived at Northwestern University, I was very uncomfortable with my fellow students' behaviors. They were wild people. Kids seem to be more sophisticated at an earlier age these days. On the Chicago campus, men outnumbered women eleven to one. I learned rather quickly that many of the young women were there for the Mrs. Degree, something which hadn't entered my mind at that point.

Being on the near north shore of Lake Michigan meant participating in the good life—lots of clubs and bars. I was such a small town girl that when I went to bars with these new friends, I drank terrible black coffee. By the second semester, I decided to join them and learned to drink beer with the best of them. I still don't like it.

I studied two years at Northwestern University's school of business. I spent evenings taking night classes and weekends making spending money at part time jobs.

My food allowance was $15 a week for cafeteria fare. Once I learned to smoke, I began making soup my healthy food in order to afford cigarettes. I always worked part time during both high school and college for the Protestant work ethic had been drummed into me. I still wrestle with it and feel guilty if I sit down and do nothing for a minute.

Because Dad said all Brians attended Illinois Wesleyan University, I transferred there my junior year. I joined a sorority. I was raised a Methodist when government-sanctioned segregation permeated the land. Methodist conferences (divisions) were separated by color. The southern conference was the one for Negroes. I wonder what Jesus or John Wesley would have had to say about that. To me it seems antithetical to Christianity to separate people by the color of their skin. Ministers, white guys with some modicum of education, decided to have segregated conference divisions.

At Wesleyan, I left my sorority because two young women of color from Spellman College were not allowed to stay in our sorority house while they did their 'semester abroad' in Illinois. Corporate sorority headquarters deemed young black women could not live in the same house with a bunch of white girls. This was a 'stop the world I want to get off' moment for me.

I've thought of those women over the years and have often tried to put myself in their places. That kind of hurt has to run very deep and must last forever. I imagine it still enters their minds as it does mine. Imperfect and as flawed as we are, fair treatment of all races should be the order of the day. If I had been born a black female, I imagine I would have become very angry with the world around me. I probably would not have controlled my rage and might have ended up in prison. I have gone marching through life with white privilege.

I graduated from Illinois Wesleyan University with a major in sociology and a minor in psychology. After graduation I worked in Chicago for a couple of years with a group of fifty Midwestern physicians doing clinical cancer chemotherapy research. Living at home with my family, having dinner prepared each night after work and then meeting Mark all make for pleasant memories. I went to graduate school one semester at Roosevelt, but I knew I'd never conquer calculus, so I quit while I was ahead.

Dad and I often commuted into Chicago together. Once he accused me of eating a 'whore's breakfast.' I asked what that meant, and he said, "They drink black coffee and smoke a cigarette." I asked him how he knew what whores ate for breakfast. He walked away and never brought it up again. He would have had no idea under the sun what they ate or drank for breakfast or any other meal. No way.

Another Culture Rears

This is an *olio* which happened one evening when I was waiting tables for college money. It took place the summer between my sophomore and junior years. These were the days before 'servers' introduced themselves to customers. The conversation went something like this:

"Hi there, Cutie! What's your name?"

Always hoping for a good tip, I was friendly and told him, because I didn't relish the name "Cutie." "How old are you, eh?"

I told him that too. Of course, I was quick-witted enough to ask how old he was. *Too old and 'sophisticated' for me for sure,* I thought. *I'm still a kid.*

He was a ruddy, handsome guy—*with a 'build' only hard work brings,* I mused. With a full head of wavy brown hair and blue eyes shining bright against a tanned face, he was very sophisticated looking for 28 years of age. *Better keep my distance,* I warned myself.

That was my introduction to the hard working, but not necessarily well educated, strong men who dug and built natural gas pipelines all across some states in our lower 48 to Alaska. This monumental work, done way back in the late fifties in northern Illinois, has enriched our lives enormously, while most of us don't even recognize it.

I learned this 'career path' when I waited tables at the biggest restaurant in Naperville. They did a land-office kind of business serving noteworthy 'specials'—like 'all the spaghetti you can eat for

74

a buck.' Once a sleepy little town, now it is the second largest city in the state after Chicago. Most every imaginable cuisine is available there today.

Still sitting in a booth after the restaurant closed, the poor lonely 'boy' regaled the other waitresses and me with stories. I remember just this one:

"Danger lurks everywhere in our work," he began. *Perhaps this was to serve as a chick magnet,* I'm thinking now. On the other hand, working with natural gas had to be an extremely dangerous occupation.

He went on to recount, "Men are sometimes mangled by machinery."

He talked about the weather—especially Illinois mid-summer thunderstorms and the resulting water-soaked earth which made digging so difficult. Additionally, heat from that unrelenting sun (then through less polluted skies) and glacial rocks (embedded for millennia) were everyday obstacles.

He began, "One day fire erupted."

This pipeline cowboy's suave demeanor reversed itself, and with a panic stricken expression on his face, that smooth 'cool' left him. His face became contorted. Sweat appeared on his brow, and he resembled something of the proverbial deer caught in headlights. The tough guy image evaporated.

"Fire!" several men hollered. Panic ensued.

"Where?" others screamed.

"Over here, over there," several men cried at once.

Cries of impending death were heard from obscenities filling the air.

"Where the hell is that fire extinguisher? Shit. We've gotta put out this damn fire."

In a little bitty voice they eventually heard, "I've got it," from the skinny, pimply-faced rookie kid on the crew. "It's *ry-cheer.*"

"What do it say, boy?" they shouted all at once.

The boy frightened beyond words looked down again at the bright, spanking new fire extinguisher.

"What do it say, boy?" losing any patience left, they screamed at him again and again.

He drawled, 'Made in *Chi-cargo*'.

The poor kid found the origins of the fire extinguisher but was way too rattled to read any directions.

The teller of the tale burst out laughing at that point thinking this was a very funny story. The smooth guy returned. This tragedy obviously was averted, because I would have heard if it were still ablaze.

Are pipeline cowboys are still on the loose around the world—digging pipelines by day and preying on innocent young women with their stories of bravery after hours? Of course, they are! Just look, young cuties. Keep your distance, but listen to their stories—their funny, exaggerated stories.

From OREOS *to* OLIOS

PART II

Mr. Right and Then…

I'll begin with the fork in the road, and yes, I took the right one. Yogi Berra once said, "When you meet a fork in the road, take it." I did, and here's what happened.

The date was April 14, 1963. It was Easter. Terrible things were happening throughout the world. Something important had happened to me. I had turned 24 a week earlier. A few significant events had taken place before then, but my life changed forever that night.

It was a long way from northern Illinois on that Good Friday when Dr. Martin Luther King wrote his essay entitled, 'Letter from the Birmingham Jail.' This letter would become an important piece of our American history.

Although events of great consequence were taking place, I was getting ready for the 'young professionals' mixer' at the Illinois Athletic Club in Chicago. I'd never done mixers like this before, but a friend from work said it was a good place to meet interesting people (unattached professional men). She would go with me as she wanted to meet some too. I felt I knew all the charming people I could handle, but there was no husband material in the lot.

I had moved back home to live with Mom and Dad the previous December still recovering from a jolting experience with 'love.' I went in my new hairdo, a curly permanent. I also wore what I thought was the latest fashion, a white polyester sleeveless blouse with matching pleated skirt both covered in blue carnations. That was before flowers were dyed blue. I have since learned that flowers belong on wallpaper—not people.

We met at Union Station and took the 157 bus over to Michigan Avenue. That has been my lucky number for over 50 years—157. It was the same bus I had taken from the train station to my dorm at Abbott Hall my first two years of college. It would become my little brother's police patrol car number in later years.

Arriving at the elegant athletic club, we found the ballroom full of both beautiful and not-so-beautiful people. I sat at a table with parapsychologists from the University of Chicago, and my friend danced. I met some unusual people, but I didn't comprehend a thing they discussed.

Finally after a long time, my friend and her dance partner joined us. Since I hadn't been asked to dance by any of those University of Chicago folks, I decided to take a chance on her dancer and asked, "Do you know how to jitterbug?" as that was what the band was gearing up for.

"Of course," he said. "Let's dance!" And we did.

After a couple of dances, we returned to the table, and I took my friend aside to ask her if she was interested in this guy. Her answer was, "No, he's not my type."

Of course, we couldn't have known what type he was at that time, but after a bit more conversation, I learned that he lived just two suburbs east of my town. He was in the Army but was allowed to wear civilian clothes when off duty. He would be happy to drive me home.

Drive me home? I'd never gotten into a car with someone I didn't know before. Being a sensible young woman, I asked to see some of his identification. I decided to copy down all the numbers from his identification. I told my friend I knew I was taking a chance riding home with this person, but he seemed nice enough and was going my way, 25 miles west of the City.

She grinned and said, "Hey, maybe you'll find him exciting! That's what we came for, remember?"

She held onto the scribbled notes of his identity. In case he turned out to be a cold blooded killer, she could inform the police if I didn't show up for work the next morning.

So off we went. Before we got down the steps from the Chicago Athletic Club to the sidewalk, I knew the following: He had a name, Mark; his younger brother David was married a year ago right out of college, and he and his wife Rosemary were expecting in August; his parents were divorced when he was five; his mother and grandmother lived in Fort Lee, New Jersey; he graduated from Bowling Green State University in Ohio; now he worked on an Army missile site at Argonne National Laboratory as a First Lieutenant and had orders to Thule, Greenland. Off we went in his little Austin Healy Sprite sports car. As I recall, he didn't have a quarter for the toll way, so I tossed in one of mine. We got home to Sunset Drive, and I invited him in for fresh coffee and stale donuts. The rest is history. I wouldn't be going back to another young professionals' mixer.

"He's always clean and takes you nice places." This was Mom's take on my new boyfriend a few weeks later. I wonder what I had been dragging home if this was her pronouncement on Mark. She was right. He had two shirts, both green. He alternated wearing them, and they were always clean and pressed. And he did take me nice places.

We heard some great Dixieland jazz, on one date and took in Second City, a popular improvisational theater club, on another. He told me the plots of all the recent books he had read. He fed me well in great restaurants. I was beginning to like this guy.

He had a lieutenant friend who wanted to double date with us, so we went to Hugh Hefner's Playboy Club, the original one, in Chicago. He arrived to pick me up rather late during a downpour. Before he got the top back up on that sports car, he was soaking wet, so he looked rather drippy. He asked Mom if he could use her iron, and down he went to the family room, took off his clothes and ironed them dry. Don't you think any mom would have loved that ingenuity? Mine talked about it for years.

Little brother Mike early on in our courtship hid behind bushes covered in white sheets near the front door and jumped out at Mark asking, "Are you here to see my *seester*?"

Mark allowed as how he was, and then Mike informed him that he was a secret agent, and told him, "Go on in." It's a wonder Mark ever came back for more. Later, Mark decided it would be a good thing to take our own personal secret agent on dates with us once in awhile. I wonder if Mike remembers any of our dates.

It turns out that Dad and Mark had almost everything in common. They both loved classical music, reading and learning. Both were liberal Democrats, left of center. I didn't realize then how much they were alike. I'd found a winner in everybody's eyes. The only way Mark and Dad differed was that Mark wasn't addicted to chocolate or cigars.

Falling in Love

We had a whirlwind courtship. We were engaged in August at Rockefeller Point on the Hudson River with a family heirloom diamond ring which had belonged to his grandmother, Blanche Gilman (Gani). I met his mom and grandmother then, and they approved. Mark then left for Greenland for the first part of his tour of duty.

I learned during our dating that he did things differently from most young men I had known. During his high school prom, he went swimming in Brooklyn with his buddies instead of dancing. Yes, that was a cheaper way to spend the evening.

He celebrated Thanksgiving with Chinese food. While visiting his mother and grandmother in Fort Lee, New Jersey, on that holiday, he took them out for dinner driving them one at a time in his little Austin Healy Sprite. My life just took on a most interesting twist. A thought ran through my head…*maybe I'd never have to produce Thanksgiving dinner—the whole turkey deal.*

As he was putting the ring on my finger, he promised he would take me to the capitals of the world: London, Paris, Madrid and Rome in that order. What girl would have said 'no' to that?

He talked about the Foreign Service retirement plan. I didn't know then that retirement plans were important. He already was considering them. Here I am now enjoying his early research and prescience on retirement.

One more thing from our courtship—which I'm free to write

about—is that he loved to tell me the plots of all the books he read. It looked as if I might never read again—I had a built in book reporter. His language facility was superb, so the stories came alive with his telling. I could just listen. I didn't have to worry about carrying on a scintillating conversation.

I never did get to live in any of those world capitals, but I did visit them all and was lucky to have multiple visits to some.

While in Greenland, he called weekly, and we sent each other small reel-to-reel tapes so we could 'talk'. We were both taking guitar lessons, so we'd play our guitars for one another and sing protest songs of the day. "If I had a Hammer," "We Shall Overcome," and "John Henry" are three tunes I recall belting as I hunted for the right chords. Early into his Thule tour, he sent me a lengthy tape saying when he came home on leave in March we should get married.

The sun went down and darkness enveloped his missile base the day President John F. Kennedy was assassinated. That was a difficult time for both of us. I remember making him a tape, unable to talk, so mostly he just heard me crying. Mark's news arrived by short wave radio, and his New York Times newspapers were often weeks late, but they heard about the Kennedy assassination immediately—national security, you know. What a bleak time for us all.

Of course we weren't together at Christmas. I was inundated with gifts anyhow—I never have received so much loot. He signed different peoples' names to gifts so it wouldn't look like I was being spoiled by just one person.

Here's a partial list: Robert Kennedy sent me pearl earrings, which I still wear. Ambassador McCloskey (our envoy to Ireland whom I must have thought was rather cute) sent me a Japanese tea set. A gold watch came from some other well known person—it may have been Johnny Carson—I can't remember for sure. I still wear the opal earrings which were part of that booty. I lost the pendant on the Paris metro a few years ago. I hope someone is enjoying it as much as I did. A Dansk coffee service! Steak knives! A carving set! I was completely spoiled that year when he was away. We've not spent another holiday season apart which is the only Christmas gift I need.

In early March he managed to get on the last plane out of Thule before a storm grounded all aircraft for weeks. The arctic storm set in and didn't end until weeks after the wedding. What would I have done on March 7 when people were gathered for the wedding and the groom didn't show up because he had been snowed in? I wonder if that's a good enough excuse for not showing up for one's wedding.

A co-worker helped me pick out my perfect lace wedding suit. Years later when it no longer fit, a Dutch friend suggested, "Make that skirt into a pillow. You have the husband, who needs the dress?" So I did, but a lace pillow made from the skirt never quite fit into our home's décor.

About 100 friends and family attended our wedding held in the Wesley United Methodist Church in Naperville, Illinois. The wedding was fun. I don't know if they are supposed to be so enjoyable. All four of our parents were present for the occasion. Aunts, uncles, cousins and friends attended. Looking back on it now, I see it is true that families congregate for weddings and funerals. I prefer the former.

My brother Doug had foot surgery a week before the wedding. Poor guy—he looked like he was wearing patent leather shoes, but they were really black shiny rubbers as he was unable to fit feet into shoes. Nonetheless, he was able to carry Gani upstairs on a straight back chair to the banquet hall for our dinner at Willoway Manor.

We went off to Nassau for our honeymoon. After our holiday in the sun, I returned to Illinois and to my job at the Midwest Cooperative Chemotherapy Group. Mark was to fly back to Greenland. However, because of that awful storm which was still raging, no planes were going into Thule either. He called me from Fort Dix where he waited for transportation and suggested I just come on back and wait with him. My boss gave me more leave time. We spent our extra days together in a waiting room in case the storm broke and a plane could leave. Dozens of others were waiting for flights too, but they were off to Asia and Europe and could board planes and leave. We fit in an extra honeymoon with those few added days.

He eventually did have to return to Greenland for the remainder of his unaccompanied (no wives) tour. That snowstorm could have lasted forever, and I would have been much happier. I cried all the way back to Chicago.

I set about entertaining myself buying second hand furniture for our apartment-to-be. It kept me busy on the weekends when I wasn't working. I involved the whole family in painting the new used furniture green. No style matched any other, but everything was the same color and looked great after antiquing. I already had the maple bedroom set from my 16th birthday, so for a total of $200, I furnished our first apartment.

My great Aunt Alice made us a crazy quilt for our wedding. It was stolen during our only move with the Army, but we have a photograph of the quilt in our wedding album to remember it by.

Dumped?

Early in our married life, Mark lost me. Clearly, he said, "Sandy, I'll be back here to pick you up within an hour. Wait on that park bench, right there. See the one?"

We were at the US Capitol building in Washington, DC. I had my resume in my tight little fist ready to apply for a job in a Senate office which probably needed me.

I had heard about the Senate Democratic Policy Committee on Capitol Hill from one of the physicians I had worked with. He advised me I might be able to find a job with them when I moved to the area. He had been the elevator boy for Lyndon B. Johnson's personal elevator when LBJ was the Senate majority leader while working his way through medical school.

Being naïve even at 25, I thought I'd just go ahead and take them a resume. The doctor who gave me the lead didn't have any connections to them. "Just say you're a Democrat."

Mark had returned from his tour in Greenland and was assigned to Fort Meade, Maryland. Now, we were actually beginning our lives together. His mother and grandmother were visiting us in our first apartment in Laurel, Maryland, appropriately named "Mistletoe Gardens."

Gani's brother, Carl Grening, was buried in Arlington National Cemetery, so Mark drove Gani and his mom over the bridge to visit the cemetery while I dropped off my resume.

I found the office just inside the Senate side of the capitol and walked right in. A woman sitting at the desk looked up and asked the typical, "May I help you?"

I began thinking perhaps it would have been appropriate to knock on the heavy, oversized mahogany doors first. But, I was there, and there she was asking me the question, so I had to do something.

"Yes, I believe so," I stammered. I mumbled something about how I was new in the city and thought they might like to hire me since I was both an executive secretary and a Democrat.

"Here's my resume," I offered as I handed it over.

She acted like she didn't encounter this kind of request every day. She said, rather curtly, "We aren't hiring. We have a perfectly good secretary. Thank you for stopping by."

I was embarrassed, but I have no recollection of saying anything more than a muttered, "Thank you for your time."

Interview over. I mused, *that encounter didn't take long enough to secure a job*. I headed straight for the park bench to sit and wait for Mark to return. I felt like the unsophisticated country girl I was. I hadn't expected down time, and there I sat without a fingernail file or a book.

It was a lovely park. Nice bench. Terrific trees just beginning to show their autumn colors. I was quite content to sit there and conjure up some ideas on how I might look for another job or become a good cook or be a decent daughter-in-law. The capitol loomed large just across the street. I spent a considerable amount of time daydreaming about how wonderful life might have been had I landed that job.

I did have a watch, one of those Christmas presents. One hour went by. Then another. I sat and waited. Mark and his family didn't show up. After three hours I thought they might have had some kind of problem. Gani was quite elderly. Perhaps something had happened to her. I thought I was sitting on the right bench in the right park just across the street from the Capitol building

Late afternoon arrived. I didn't have much money. By this time, I felt very alone and frightened although there was nothing happening to frighten me. We were planning on staying in the city that night as our apartment was quite small, and we would all be more comfortable in hotel rooms. I hadn't listened closely when they discussed which hotel we'd be staying in. Our little red Volvo was no where in sight.

I headed for the Capitol Hill police station, located a few steps down under the ground in the park. A burly cop looked up when I entered. Perfectly composed, I related the whole story to him. I explained that we were newly married, and I knew my husband would be picking me up, but he must be lost or he must have had an accident or his grandmother must have taken ill. Would he please find out if something had happened to them?

The last thought I related to him was, "He wouldn't just dump me in a park. We just got married."

The cop looked up at me standing there—now with tears running down my cheeks and offered, "Lady, it happens every day."

I felt this couldn't be happening to me. Gathering my wits again, I asked if I could use his phone and phone book to start calling hotels. I looked over the list, and the Sheraton Hilton on Connecticut Avenue rang a bell. I dialed the number. Finally, luck was with me. "Yes, Mark Lore is registered here," and "Yes, I will connect you to the room."

"Where have you been?" he literally shouted into the phone.

"I'm where you told me to be. I'm in the park. I waited and sat on the bench, but you never came to pick me up."

His mother said later that he couldn't find me. Somehow or another, we mixed up our signals. Maybe I hadn't heard him correctly as I was very excited about the prospect of working for Senator Mike Mansfield. Maybe Mark couldn't find the park again. At that time, he didn't know Washington, D.C. like the back of his hand as he does now. We'll never know what really happened that day.

The hotel elevator wall got a pounding according to Mark's mom and grandmother. He frantically hit it again and again wondering what had happened to me.

The cop was wrong. That comforted me. The thought of dumping me hadn't entered Mark's head. Everything in my world was all right again. The little red Volvo soon rolled up and I was gathered in.

I don't remember another thing about our weekend in the District of Columbia. I'm usually pretty good at remembering what food I ate, but that didn't register either. Senator Robert Kennedy was giving a speech at the hotel, and Mark saw him come in and head for the speaking engagement. But, that wasn't part of my experience that day.

Monday morning we were back in our little apartment in Laurel and ready to resume our new lives. Mark went off to Fort Meade. He was a new Army Captain and had a job he disliked intensely. He said he just kicked tires all day. Mid-morning the phone rang.

"Mrs. Lore? This is Pauline Moore with the Senate Democratic Policy Committee. You stopped in last week and left your resume. I hope you haven't found another job yet. We wondered if you would like to work for us. Our secretary is pregnant and will be leaving in two weeks. My world was expanding.

When the two weeks later finally arrived, Mark delivered me to the commuter train in Laurel before he set off for Fort Meade and another day of lashing out at tires. When his day ended, he met me at the train station. Our hours meshed perfectly. Twice each day going to and from Union Station, I crossed that infamous park where Mark lost me.

A plush office with an enormous chandelier hanging from the ceiling would become my daytime environment. The floor was carpeted wall to wall. I'd never seen such large mahogany desks before.

The biggest thrill of all came on the first day of work. My office mate was Grace Tully who had been President Franklin Roosevelt's private secretary. She was with him in Warm Springs, Georgia, when he died. Although elderly by the time I worked with her, she regaled me day in and day out with stories about life in Washington, White House tales and her personal friends who happened to be the governing elite. She even knew Adlai Stevenson, my hero. Senators stopped by to visit. One brought her fresh white asparagus from California. I had never heard of white asparagus. I got paid all the while I tallied Senate votes.

The work was often boring. Miss Tully, truly a fine raconteur, made up for the dull vote counting we did. Three lawyers were housed in another, equally posh office. I typed speeches for Senator Mansfield and then ran off to the Senate Gallery to watch him read them. I loved being at a seat of power.

Mark's dad had a copy of Grace Tully's book, *FDR, My Boss,* which he gave me and which Miss Tully later autographed. She also gave me two of President Roosevelt's signatures—one when he was healthy and the other written just before he died.

Almost as soon as this job began, it ended. Mark was called to join the Foreign Service. He was to begin in January. He 'walked' his papers through the Pentagon and Fort Meade and was out of the Army and into the Foreign Service within two weeks. His tire-kicking era ended. I left what I thought might become my dream job on the Hill.

In January, 1965, Mark began his Foreign Service career. My time in the Senate Democratic Policy Committee didn't last long, but it left a lasting impression and memories of a few months which I'll always cherish.

Even today, I'll remind Mark, "Don't forget to pick me up." It's an unconscious verbal tick I haven't been able to shake. I don't want to wait and wonder if I've been dumped. I have not been lost again, yet.

Diplomacy Begins

What a 'state' to be in! After taking the four-month Diplomacy 101 course in the U.S. Department of State, the program directors for new Foreign Service officers gave out assignments. We spouses were invited for this big day. The announcer finally got to the Ls in the alphabet and read, "Mark Lore, Rio."

I had been studying the world map diligently in order to learn where the newly independent and recently partitioned African countries were located as well as their new African names. Delighted beyond words, when I heard "Mark Lore, Rio," I jumped up, screamed and let everybody in the room know that I knew its location.

Recently, I read the detailed obituary of a Foreign Service wife in the *Washington Post*. It told of various jobs she had held 'before settling into a career as a Foreign Service spouse.' I had never heard this job referred to as a career before. But, I may use her line someday when people ask what I did. Although I'm not a direct descendent of the first governor of the Plymouth Colony, I had the same career path as she did.

Soon, completely immersed, Mark was busy learning everything he'd need to know for his first job in the Foreign Service. When the new diplomats' studies weren't classified, the other spouses and I could participate. The class often went out to eat together. One time in particular, about 20 of us dined at someone's favorite Chinese restaurant. Those 'in the know' took care of ordering three large platters of food to share. Platters were passed around the table. When the squid floating in its own ink arrived, I passed it by. I don't think I uttered a sound, and I didn't stick up my nose. I just knew that food wouldn't pass my lips.

Returning home after the dinner, Mark gave me a soft spoken homily on the need to try new things. Although I spent the next 32 years trying new stuff, I never ate squid swimming in black ink. Years later during our tour in Portugal, I couldn't get enough squid (called *lulas* in Portuguese), but they were grilled and a taste delight. I never gave their ink a second thought. There's hardly anything more delicious. To my knowledge I've not eaten snakes or cats or mice.

During these introductory courses, we learned that if we were assigned to countries with chiefs and huts, our husbands might be offered the second baby bird which fell from the nest in the chief's hut. The chief because of his exalted rank would eat the first to drop, and the young diplomat would get the second. I made a mental note to stay out of huts.

We figured out how we got the assignment to Rio de Janeiro years later. Much paperwork had to be filled in before Mark ever stepped foot into 'Diplomacy 101.' While watching television in the apartment one evening, we checked off some languages we'd like to learn. When we got to the Ps, there was 'Portuguese.' We looked at each other and in unison whispered, "Ah, Sonnets from the Portuguese," poems written by Elizabeth Barrett Browning in the middle of the 19th century. We never could have imagined we would spend the next 32 years in and out of Portuguese-speaking countries just because we checked that box.

Now I'm aware of all the other languages we might have ticked off, and I'm so grateful we found the Ps first. Our lives would have taken a different course had we been taught Spanish first or some esoteric hard language like Japanese or Chinese at the beginning of Mark's career. Instead, we flew off to Rio to learn Portuguese on location.

My parents threw a big farewell party for our friends in Illinois. We have photos of the lovely flower centerpiece Mom ordered from the florist, delectable food surrounding it, and the young diplomat and his wife smiling and looking happy. My skinny dress even exudes happiness—bright orange flowers ready to meld into the tropical scene of Rio.

Dad used to ask, "Is it better to go and not be ready or to be ready and not to go?" I think we were as ready as we'd ever be. We were on our way to learn our first foreign language in Brazil. My life experiences continued to expand.

Although I was eager and looked forward to this new phase of our lives, I cried most of the way flying down to Rio. I was really leaving my family now. In addition to the white gloves and calling cards, we spouses were told to carry along black funeral suits because we would be attending many state funerals during our assignments. I wore mine. When Mark's career ended thirty-two years later, I still hadn't attended a state funeral.

We arrived at our first posting at night. I never would get directions straight after that.

Off We Go

"Estamos atterisando no Rio!" (We are landing in Rio). I felt the pangs of terror beginning. I wasn't in the USA any longer. Home—a cocoon of sorts—had disappeared. We became a tight married couple, united against the rest of the world. Apron strings were cut.

Mark was assigned to what was then the largest American Embassy in our hemisphere. Brazil itself is larger than the continental United States, so this was not an unimportant, insignificant country. Rio, celebrating its 400th anniversary, was a fabulous and exciting place to begin our Foreign Service life. I knew we would meet remarkable people along the way. What an enticing new culture awaited our discoveries.

What I learned during this first posting was that Mark needed wings to fly, and I needed roots to keep me grounded. I was thousands of miles from home. No family, friends, co-workers, neighbors. Nothing smelled like home. Nothing sounded like home. Nothing tasted like home. Culture shock attacked me with a vengeance! Nothing connected me to this place except gravity. I couldn't even read a menu until after a few hours in Portuguese-language class. Mark ordered raw hamburger for one of his early meals. Of course, we've learned since that *steak tartar* is a delicacy, but I've never eaten it. My survival in the Foreign Service depended on my making a nest for us, a respite from the outside world. I soon appreciated the old adage, "Home is where the heart is."

Rio was full of excitement and filled with sultry, beautiful people with varying shades of skin color. Flesh was in the forefront everywhere. World-class beaches were in abundance as were tropical fruits and vegetables. Fish from southern waters were another new extraordinary taste sensation. Permeating the air everywhere was Brazilian music, exhaust fumes and that strange foreign language bellowed day and night. We didn't even pay the air fare to live in that tropical paradise

On the first day in-country, getting to the Embassy from our *Regente Hotel* was a challenge. We showed the taxi driver our American passports. He didn't read English any more than we spoke Portuguese. We did finally find the location and began intensive four month language instruction the following week. We spent six hours a day being treated like babies learning a language by repeating over and over again what sounded like babble to us. We finally saw the written language after several weeks. Somehow or another, we stayed happily married. The State Department knew what it was doing issuing one-way tickets to posts. (I didn't have enough money for a ticket home).

I had never tasted avocado before dinner on our first night in Rio. Another young couple, the Petersons, invited several junior officers and their wives for dinner. I was nervous, but the evening was fun and elegant. The other people at dinner, also on their first Foreign Service tour, were no longer novices but urbane and knowledgeable since they had been living in Rio for several months.

We met Lolly and Tom at that first Rio meal. Lolly was pregnant with Ann their second child. Tom told us to feel free to ask any questions we had. I did have one overriding one.

"Tom, what is that toilet-like looking thing in our hotel bathroom? Is it to clean feet?" That was the only possible use I could imagine; after all with so many beaches, sand had to be cleaned off feet somehow.

Tom was a southern gentleman from Alabama. He turned red and seemed to be at a loss for words. "It is called a *bidet*, and I understand it is used for feminine hygiene," he muttered.

"Oh," I replied. "But it could be used for feet, too, don't you think?"

We lived in the hotel for a month before finding our Copacabana apartment. Someone on the hotel staff embroidered our name on every piece of dirty laundry so it would be returned to the rightful owners after washing. What a dull job. I was beginning to take note as to how privileged I was—a white, relatively educated North American woman.

A wonderful restaurant serving all manner of simple, local food was located right next door to the hotel, so we ate there often and were always served by Henrique Segundo. Henrique was one of three brothers, and as his parents liked the name Henrique so much, they named their first boy Henrique Primeiro, (Henry the First), then came our Henrique Segundo (Henry the Second), and finally Henrique Terceiro (Henry the Third). I never encountered that kind of fixation with one name.

Once we learned some Portuguese and Mark passed the tests, he began his rotational training in the Embassy. I got a job working for the political counselor. Although answering the phone and filing newspaper articles were good for my Portuguese, I was glad when the permanent American employee arrived at post and I could be a lady of leisure along with the other junior officers' wives.

In addition to the rules of white gloves, calling cards and black funeral suits, I would be required to pay a call on the Ambassador's wife. I was instructed to limit my visit to 15 minutes—after all, if I needed to make this call, so did every other spouse in the Embassy. My husband was the bottom guy on the totem pole. She and her husband were eminent academics from Harvard. On arrival at her residence, I learned she had no roots in Brazil either. She felt alone too. Her ivory tower in academia wasn't anything like this protocol-ridden Embassy business. She kept me for two and one half hours regaling me with what she didn't like about the Foreign Service and how much she felt like a fish out of water. After that visit, I felt my culture shock wasn't as profound as hers. And, I learned I had an innate talent, buried until now. I was a good listener.

Most wives weren't working at the Embassy, so it gave me a chance to get to know them. We had no phone, so when the doorbell rang, it was like getting a phone call before caller ID. You answered. As I recall, my new friends dropped in daily for coffee, tea and chatting.

I became the 'little match girl' at the American Women's Club (AWC) of Rio. You might think that was an easy role to play. It wasn't; I learned early on it carried a certain degree of responsibility. Many people still smoked, so the AWC sold match books as a fundraiser—bright red ones with their name imprinted on the flap. I sat there in the hallway outside the meeting room selling matches and bridge tally cards before the meetings began. I saw everyone who entered.

At one point the Embassy hosted a high powered delegation from the United States to the Organization for American States conference, and Mrs. Dean Rusk, wife of the Secretary of State, gave an address to the American Women's Club. I was able to meet Mrs. Rusk, Mrs. Frank Church, wife of the Senator from Idaho, and Mrs. Hugh Scott, wife of the Senator from Pennsylvania before that meeting began. Mrs. Rusk treated our gathering like she was having a talk with a few close women friends rather than several hundred strangers. She told us about the families of the President's cabinet and how the wives coped being married to men working in important government positions. She almost broke down when talking about Jacqueline Kennedy, the young widow.

Just before this event began, a woman stormed up to the table where I was sitting and demanded, "Do you know who I am?"

I didn't recognize her and admitted as much. The woman told me her name and added that she was the wife of the Deputy Chief of Mission, and whenever I saw her enter a room, I should stand up. *God Almighty!* I thought…*I'm in the Foreign Service now!* Of course, I stood up, but I didn't salute. I don't think she mentioned saluting.

I know one stands for the President or his emissary and women older than you are—not for some guy's wife although she was older than I. Everybody was.

At Thanksgiving in 1965, Robert Kennedy and his entourage were in Rio. A group of us was standing outside the 'stage door' before Mr. Kennedy reached the throng of people waiting to see him in front of the building where he had spoken. He shook my hand and wished me a Happy Thanksgiving. Two years ago on this very date, his brother,

President Kennedy, was assassinated. His blue eyes held such a depth of sadness. Mine could not hide the tears.

Averill Harriman also visited Rio during this time. Because I've always been a groupie of one sort or another, I wrote home about these high level visitors. Dad wrote, "Hope you also saw Mr. Harriman. He is quite a guy really, although not getting any younger. These rich people with social vision deserve the plaudits of all." How true.

We ate a great variety of excellent food in Rio. Prior to this assignment, we figured the best fare in the world was Howard Johnson's fried clams. Although we didn't have quite enough money to make it from the beginning of the month until the end, when we felt flush, we ate fabulous food only a block from our Copacabana apartment. I especially remember beef stroganoff—an enormous portion made with filet mignon practically filled your plate—easily it could have fed a family of four. It was served with rice and French fried potatoes. Brazilians still do that—give you two starches—because both are delicious.

After a month in the hotel, we moved to an elegant apartment in Copacabana. This area of Rio held about 700,000 people at the time, so most housing was in high rise apartment buildings. We inherited a maid named Hilda from an employee leaving Rio for Algiers. I thought Hilda was quite a character—perhaps because she's the first maid I'd ever employed. I came home with some Aunt Jemima pancake mix from the commissary one day, and she informed me Aunt Jemima was Brazilian. There was no telling her any different.

Hilda was born somewhere in the middle of a family of 23 children, but only seven had survived into adulthood. Her dad was 72 when the last child was born and then up and died at 73. None of the kids went to school, but her parents taught the children to read. She learned English in night school and had dreams of becoming a practical nurse so she could work at Strangers Hospital (the one which takes care of us foreigners or *estrangeiros*).

Hilda had never used a washing machine before and was used to hand washing all dirty laundry. Our wringer washer made the trip from the United States to Brazil upside down which meant oil leaked all over it, and new parts had to be ordered from the states. Mom and Dad shipped us the needed parts from Sears. Hilda still could not keep herself from wringing out the clothes by hand before she put them through the washer's wringer. She loved the stove and refrigerator, also brought from the states (but shipped upright) in that cool copper tone color of that era.

It was necessary to have a maid in Rio. Without one, I could never have left the kitchen or laundry area. Water had to be boiled for drinking and food preparation. It was safe to eat lettuce and other fresh produce only at home after it had been soaked in iodine and water, rinsed, soaked in a bleach solution for 20 minutes and then thoroughly rinsed with boiled, filtered water. Time consuming was an understatement. It still probably contained some germs or vermin—but we hoped most dangerous bugs were killed with one mixture or another.

We bought our first furniture in Rio. For the total sum of $425 we purchased a buffet and harvest table with six chairs. It was all so well built, I'm guessing it will still be around at least another 200 years or so if the family takes care of it.

Early in December we met a nice German couple on the beach. The husband was also a diplomat, and although his wife was a pediatrician, she had given up her career in medicine to follow him in the Foreign Service—wherever that might take them. They invited us to 'come by' to their apartment on Boxing Day, December 26. This was our first Christmas away from home, and we filled our time with people, parties and invitations to our apartment.

December 26 arrived, and we ate healthy portions of borscht at a Russian restaurant before heading to our new German friends' apartment. Arriving there, we were presented with a roast beef dinner and all the trimmings. Remember, these were Germans, so there were many trimmings. We didn't think we had been invited for dinner, but we both tried to eat like we were hungry. From then on, I asked for more information when invited to someone's home to make sure I didn't double dip again into more than one dinner per evening.

We were told before leaving the United States that Brazilians were not fond of pets. However, it seemed to me every other person on the street in Copacabana was being led by a dog or two. Brazilians were not cat lovers, but then, most cats stayed indoors. One Sunday afternoon we made a trip to a city park and we found hundreds of feral cats roaming around. Mark told his Portuguese teacher about our discovery the next day, and Luis advised him about another park which hosted not only feral cats but also the world's largest rodents with black stripes down their backs. We decided to let that park go. After all, there was no way we could see everything Rio had to offer.

I conversed in English with a young female physician every Saturday morning for a few hours during our year in Rio. She had planned a trip to New York and wanted to be understood, so we worked on her language skills for several months. Additionally, I helped take care of babies at an orphanage for 800 children on Mondays when I wasn't in language class or working in the political section. I was interested in adopting a baby, but a friend had inquired about this and learned you had to be Catholic, 40 years old and have $100,000 in the bank. We weren't close to meeting any criteria.

One day, the Embassy administrative officer called Mark in to tell him we were to be transferred to the new capital city of Brasilia. Mark was ready to go, because he knew more opportunities awaited a junior officer out in the hinterland in the small Embassy office than in the burgeoning building in Rio. The Vatican and Portugal were already represented there, and the United States wasn't far behind.

After a remarkable year in Rio, we embarked on our tour in Brasilia, the brand new city built 1,200 miles inland to move the population away from the coast and toward the middle of the country. Building a new capital in the middle of the land broke the bank; many thousands from the northeast, the poorest part of Brazil, moved to Brasilia to build a new city.

The Little Red Volvo
in Rio and Brasilia

This is the first of the car stories—same car, two stories. Mark and I had shipped our cute little red Volvo to Brazil. Six months after our arrival in Rio, the car still hadn't arrived. Mark finally asked the administrative section in the Embassy for their advice. It was, "Go look for it on the dock." And, there it was just waiting to be found; apparently, it had been sitting there for months. He was able to retrieve it within a few days.

Mark always loved an adventure, so we drove to the Embassy office in Brasilia. Not too many people made the trip on the double lane highway from metropolitan Rio de Janeiro to the new capital city which was still rather raw and relatively uninhabited. The distance was approximately the same as from New York to Chicago. We were foolhardy when I think back on it. We stopped for gas whenever we saw a gas station, and we paused to eat whenever we saw a cafe. Both were few and far between.

In Brasilia we were ensconced in an apartment building with everybody else in the Embassy office which was called by its number, *cento e treze* (113). There was a tremendous view from the living room wall of windows of the eight lanes of highway in front of the building and across the savanna as far as your eyes could see. No pollution existed then. Few cars drove on the highway. The blue skies were filled with puffy white clouds day in and day out. Against the red clay and dust, they looked bluer than usual. We did not stay there long enough to experience the rainy season. Red dust from construction swirled around everywhere. It landed on all horizontal surfaces all the time, 24/7. It was omnipresent. A maid was a necessity unless I wanted to spend all my time dusting red dirt or cleaning vegetables and boiling water.

There was little to do in Brasilia during those early days. One of my favorite activities was watching the arrival and departure of twice weekly Pan Am planes across the tundra from the apartment building. Another activity, was watching Mark drive home from the office. He went past the airport, turned right and then drove a mile or so to the apartment. After lunch, I'd watch him drive back. The bright little red car, although not a 'bug,' could always be spotted against Brasilia's clay soil. When we returned 30 years later, a bridge had been built across the manmade lake so cars heading to numbered apartment buildings wouldn't have to pass the airport enroute.

The wife of the principal officer, who was the person in charge of the Embassy office, came to me one day with a plan—she didn't call it that—she called it a wonderful opportunity. I wonder how much time she devoted to finding all us young wives something to keep us sane. She suggested I give weekly English lessons to a young person whose mother wanted her to speak English.

By this time, some of the Brazilian government had moved out to Brasilia from Rio. The President of Brazil, General Castello Branco, a widower, resided in the new city too. His daughter served as his official hostess, and it was she who wanted her 15-year-old daughter, Maria Luisa, to learn English. She asked our Embassy office if someone could give her daughter conversation classes. I was the chosen volunteer.

Maria Luisa came to our apartment every Thursday afternoon for what seemed like years, but we only lived in Brasilia six months. Being a typical teenager with an attitude, she wasn't at all interested in learning English. It began to look like a new career was unfolding for me—English conversation classes. When Maria Luisa's mother

103

learned we were being transferred to Angola, she invited me to lunch at the Presidential Palace along with a several dozen other spouses—the wives of the members of the Brazilian Congress.

This was my first invitation to a Presidential Palace. I wore my best outfit with matching new shoes for the affair. The shoes squeaked when I walked, but, never mind, they fit and went well with the new petit point beige and pink suit Mom had sent me for special occasions. And, on the appointed day, Mark came home from the office to drive me to the Presidential Palace for my brief time amongst the rich and famous.

Sleek shimmering black chauffeur-driven cars lined up in front of the palace and deposited their important cargo, the wives of the congressmen and senators. The chauffeurs didn't even have to open the car doors for their passengers. Armed guards were posted every eight to ten feet along the road and up the ramp to the palace door, so those stationed at the road opened the limo doors. Our little red Volvo rolled up. A kindly guard opened the door to let me out. My shoes began to squeak. He smiled then looked down at my shoes. I wanted to fall through some of that expensive marble right then and there.

What happened next might have been even more unusual than a luncheon guest being delivered in a little red car rather than a sleek black limousine. The soldiers could hear me coming. In fact, their heads turned as they heard my squeaky shoes approaching. They all smiled at me. I wanted to be someplace else. Anyplace else.

Luckily, the luncheon turned out to be enjoyable—helped by the fact that we sat down and nobody had to listen to my shoes. I spent the whole time conversing in Portuguese about the wonderful progress Maria Luisa had made with her English lessons, how much my husband and I had enjoyed living in their new capital and how exciting it would be to now live in Africa. Hyperbole all.

Mark picked me up at the appointed time after lunch. Both modes of transportation had made it through the day—the bright red car and the squeaky shoes. Had I been invited back to the Presidential Palace for lunch during our last tour in Brazil 30 years later, I would have arrived in a sleek, black chauffeur driven car with my husband's driver, Jesse. Had I been driven in our personal car, the dark blue Brazilian Volkswagen, it would have looked just like the hundreds of thousands of cars clogging every eight-lane highway in the town. Although a planned city, Brasilia grew like Topsy.

Moving On Again

We're going to move again! After only a year in Rio and six months in Brasilia, the United States Government (USG) developed plans to ship us to Angola. Enormously irritated about the move, I hadn't yet adjusted to living in Brazil. They spoke Portuguese in Angola, too, and Mark would have a more responsible job. Was anyone back at the Department of State concerned about the disruption in our lives? We were uprooted for the third time in eighteen months. I wondered if I could be so flexible for the rest of my life.

Lorraine, the principal officer's wife, who was the same woman who found me the opportunity for English conversation with the President's granddaughter, came to visit me and shared my concern along with some useful information. I'll always be grateful to her. First, she reminded me, "No matter where we go in the Foreign Service, there will be people, and wherever there are people, life is interesting." That was wise advice for a rather frightened, young Foreign Service wife. Mark had signed onto worldwide service, and I had signed onto Mark.

Additionally, she taught me how to organize food for dinner parties no matter where we lived. She had managed to develop menus from one continent to the next. I've always enjoyed most kinds of food. She shared all cocktail-hour food recipes.

As Foreign Service spouses, we were told how important our contributions were in representing the United States abroad. We took it seriously. I tried to keep our home looking American, and I made an effort to serve American food. There were many challenges. Often the market didn't carry what the recipe wanted.

This senior wife told me to learn what food is available in each season in whatever country we were living in. Now, here in the United States, we can buy all food in all seasons since it is shipped around the world for our demanding, voracious appetites. Back then, we bought what had been grown locally and produced dinner parties. We often dealt with exquisite fresh local fish. That was not a hardship.

After discovering what food was available, I was told to make a list of possible dinner party combinations. What was most important about this whole exercise was that I developed a cross-referenced list. Especially in small posts where you were more than likely to entertain the same 'elite' most of the time, you wouldn't want to serve them exactly the same thing time and time again.

Thus, menus were numbered. People and the date of the dinner party were listed. If Couple X got number one menu in July, you'd better be sure they got number two or three in September if they were invited again. As I recall, I worked with four or five menus in most countries. Once we landed in Europe, I could fix anything anytime. In Brussels the natives were born with sophisticated palettes and demanded fresh food from all over the globe.

Cross referencing and numbered menus developed into a great system. I shared it with all my friends so they could sail smoothly through entertaining too. I stopped using it when we left the Foreign Service. I could use that organizational tool these days, even though I produce fewer dinner parties.

You might not think any of the above information is important. But, we were big fish in little ponds during Mark's career in the Foreign Service. Later, I'll relate a story about this big fish business.

Many adventures were packed into those six months in the Brazilian hinterland. I won't write about the snakes and animals found on location and stuck into the indigenous zoo. Some snakes hung from trees even. If memory serves me correctly, some were a foot in diameter. Never mind. I don't want to write about them. That may be an exaggeration.

Although Brazilians were much more accessible in Brasilia than they were in Rio, the members of Congress left on Thursdays and returned the following Tuesday. They all went home to Rio or Sao Paulo or anyplace else in the country, because Brasilia wasn't such a great place to live. We didn't have that option.

There were two restaurants we frequented in Brasilia during this time. One was Italian, and the other one had no particular identity. Whenever we left the other one, we came home and vomited. But, it was an alternative restaurant, so we did eat there once in awhile. Finally, it sank in that it was a complete waste of money to eat dinner out only to come home and upchuck.

Mark was dealing with additional tribulations. One time the whole waiting room of the consular section was filled with nuns in habits waiting to get new passports. They all came in the same day from their mission station. Mark at the time described it to me as 'a whole sea of penguins.' Because the Embassy had only a half dozen passports on hand, the diplomatic courier was sent to Rio to pick up more.

Mark also chased down a former consul general, Cecil Cross, who had disappeared someplace in Brazil. He had retired from the United States Foreign Service and married a younger Brazilian woman and bought a ranch in the interior. The only hitch was that she had a miscreant son who wanted the ranch and instigated a plot against Mr. Cross' life. Mark and others on the search team had lots of territory to cover in search of one man. Mark found him, and upon being discovered, Mr. Cross exclaimed, "My God, I'm glad to see the Foreign Service still finds its man!" That story had a happy ending.

My adventures were not as spectacular. Each wife (at that time we were all female dependent spouses) had the pleasure of making 17 cakes for a big charity fair held each year. Each country represented (and there were very few in those years) sold its wares. I don't remember attending the fair. I do remember the hours of mixing cakes. They were frosted too. Once as a kid, I got an unfrosted angel food birthday cake when we were away from home on my birthday, and I never let my mom forget it. All angel food cakes need frosting.

Actually, I think it's the only part of an angel food cake worth eating.

Leaving Brasilia was traumatic, but not because we were leaving many friends. We hadn't been there long enough to make friends. A *despidida* (farewell party) was held for us by a Brazilian diplomat. Having always loved chocolate, I ate the wonderful chocolate mousse which was served as dessert. Fruit salad was always offered, but I couldn't pass up the mousse. Had I known what would ensue, I would have enjoyed the fruit salad so much more. I became very ill.

A local pediatrician diagnosed food poisoning. Raw eggs in the mousse were the culprit. We had already 'packed out' of our apartment and were living in temporary quarters at the Embassy because we were leaving the post. The doctor prescribed some very large pills used for rheumatism which would kill the pain. I thought they were too big to swallow and decided not to try.

Finally, after a few days of gross vomiting, diarrhea and awful grief, the Embassy called in the Peace Corps doctor from the hinterland who told me the pills might have been disastrous. I finally got well enough to travel. My weight dropped about 15 pounds—the positive result of that particular food poisoning.

Brasilia wasn't the happiest post we served in. I had my share of growing pains during our first and second assignments in Brazil. By the time we got to Angola, I felt I had some experience—I was now a seasoned wife and skinny to boot!

Another Trip

Our Rio embassy opted to send us by the 'cheapest' route from Brazil to Angola. But, traveling through Africa, the trip would take almost two weeks to get there. We would have to wait for a weekly plane in some places. Mark made a fuss about the fact that flights from Brasilia to Lisbon and onto Luanda were daily occurrences. Why couldn't we travel that route?

The Congolese dictator, General Mobuto bailed us out. When his thugs attacked the Portuguese embassy in Kinshasa, the air link to Angola was suspended requiring travel through Lisbon.

So, for the first lap of the trip, we flew from Brasilia to Rio where our friends, the Fergusons, met us. We had dinner with them, and they accompanied us to our Lisbon-bound plane. Approximately 18 people were flying from Rio to Lisbon that night—each person would be entitled to about two dozen seats, but the Varig staff decided that our little cocker spaniel Pele was overweight baggage. The dog would cost $100 to ship. We didn't have $100. This was before plastic credit cards could be produced for purchases. Luckily, our friends had the money so we got to take our dog along.

Pele would stay in the hotel with us in Lisbon as he was housetrained. That's exactly what Mark told the desk clerk at the *Eduardo VII* Hotel in Lisbon when we arrived to stay several days. "Our little dog is completely trained and never has accidents."

At that point, something in the air made us turn around to see that our little dog had a big problem with diarrhea—right there in the middle of the enormous carpet in the middle of the hotel lobby. Like us, he was nervous about flying off to new countries. The staff let us stay in spite of Pele.

We resided in the hotel for a few days while Mark consulted with the Embassy staff about Portugal's Angolan province. By this time, after 18 months of speaking almost nonstop Portuguese, I was comfortable with the language, so I had a good time touring the city while Mark worked. Lisbon is one of my favorite European cities— probably because later we were able to live there for four years in the mid 1980s. Even then in 1966, I felt I knew the territory and could pretend I belonged there. We left with our tummies full of fabulous Portuguese seafood which we had gorged on for several days.

An Undiscovered Paradise

We made it! We landed in Luanda, the capital city of Angola, where about a half million people lived. Angola is just below the big hump of Africa, under the Congo, (now called Zaire). It is a huge, rich country, twice the size of Texas.

We were picked up by the deputy consul general of the four-man consulate. He delivered us straight to our home on Avenida Cabral Moncada. It was drizzling, but we found the gardener Francisco watering the grass and plants anyway. I suppose if it's your day to work in the garden and it's the day to water, one waters whether or not it is raining. I pointed out the rain to him, and he smiled. We did have a very good relationship during our tour there. I let him do his thing. Three feet tall, prolific dahlias were his specialty. He also threw zinnia seeds at the ground. Hundreds of flowers emerged in great profusion forming a multi-colored carpet of vibrant petals.

The white stucco house with its terra cotta tiled roof resembled a space ship about to take off. We must have felt it lacked any personality, because we don't have many photos of the place.

The deputy consul general pointed out that he had left us some dry soup mix which would hold us until the maid could fix us a meal. We had flown thousands of miles for dry soup mix for lunch.

Maria Natalia had been the maid for our predecessors and waited for our arrival although everybody else in the Consulate wanted to hire her. She enriched our Luanda days more than she'll ever know. The day of our arrival, she was waiting for us at the house. She asked if we would like roast beef, green beans and fried potatoes for dinner. That was perhaps her favorite menu. Off she went to buy the ingredients. I don't think we ever added water to that dried soup mix.

We arrived in October. Thanksgiving was just around the corner. No one invited us to Thanksgiving dinner although we were new arrivals without any of our personal possessions in place yet. I understand the rest of the Consulate personnel had dinner together. Perhaps they didn't have enough plates to include us. I think, rather, they just didn't think. Mark's memory is that he told people we were going to look at a new dam site and planned to take along a picnic. I could have skipped the dam for some turkey and dressing.

Maria Natalia took it upon herself to make us a lunch which would substitute for a special dinner. Fried chicken and squash cookies were on the menu. The cookies were to remind us of pumpkin pie. After that incident, I always invited people to eat with us on Thanksgiving when we were serving overseas. At our last Thanksgiving dinner in Brasilia in 1994, we had 56 guests along with a good sized staff to pull it off.

Maria Natalia arrived at seven each morning to make our breakfast. During breakfast, after our first swig of coffee, she would ask what we would like for dinner and then tell us what we would be eating. We went through this charade every morning for two years. She was an excellent cook, the best housekeeper I've ever known and a dear friend by the time we left that post. She left work at nine p.m. after scrubbing the kitchen floor. She didn't work on Sunday. We were about the same age, and she could do everything better than I could. I've never encountered a better worker or a better non-American friend overseas. I could fill a book with the good advice and plain sense she shared with me. She calls us every Christmas from Oporto, Portugal where she lives now with her oldest sister Matilde.

One never knew in those years in Angola what might happen next. Anti-colonial guerilla fighters were active as close as 20 miles outside of town, European mercenaries surfaced at the old 17th century fort waiting to invade the Congo, and rampant rumors were the order of the day. Some were based on fact—others were made of whole cloth. There was a fragile peace between races and between people of differing political sympathies living in Luanda.

Maria Natalia was tough and not easily ruffled. She had come to Angola along with a half dozen of her siblings to secure a better life than they had been dealt in northern Portugal. The oldest brother came first and was a successful undertaker and funeral home entrepreneur. One by one, over several years' time, the rest of the family arrived at this African province of Portugal. Maria Natalia and her sister were the last to arrive. Left at home was her sister's twin, the parents' caretaker.

"Senhora, Senhora," Maria Natalia screamed from the downstairs. She took the stairs two by two to reach the main floor of the house as quickly as she could. From the look on her face, it was obvious something traumatic had taken place. I had never seen her rattled before.

"What in the world has happened?" I was accustomed to having clothes stolen from the line or lost drunks dropping by to sleep on the patio underneath the house.

Maria Natalia's face seemed to be frozen in grief and then, the story poured from her lips. With arms flailing and tears streaming down her face, she told me a young Angolan woman in agonizing pain had tried to enter the military hospital. Her husband was in the Army fighting with the Portuguese, but because she was an African, she had no right to use that hospital, and they turned her away. She slowly descended the long flight of steps. Our house was at least a mile from the hospital, and she could walk no further by the time she reached the gate to our garden. She entered and fell to the ground. Maria Natalia found her lying there. She had aborted her baby.

Maria Natalia could not be quieted. Sobbing and shaking, she cried, "The baby is dead. I found a bag to put the baby in. The woman took her baby, and I gave her some money for cab fare home."

I tore out of the house and ran up the street to find the woman but to no avail. I ran in the other direction. No luck there either. The woman must have already found a cab to return her home—her dead baby in a sack clutched tightly to her breast.

That was a heartbreaking moment, and one we'll not forget. There were other times which were nothing short of joyous, however, like our trip to Sa' da Bandeira in southern Angola. We drove to Benguela and then took the train to Sa' da Bandeira where we stayed in a lovely residential hotel.

The hotel was so residential that the guests left their bottles of wine on the table each night to await the next meal. Except for us. We were so eager to drink milk that we asked the hotel personnel to please find us some. They did, but we had to ask them to keep it refrigerated so it wouldn't spoil. As it was, everyone in the dining room seemed to watch the waiter deliver the cold milk to accompany our meals. We were green, unworldly and thirsty for milk.

Mark had to travel into the bush to Angola's southern border, so I stayed in the hotel to organize recipes and felt it wouldn't have been particularly safe for me as a foreigner to be out walking the streets unaccompanied. That's the last time recipes were organized.

On the return trip, by chance we met a kind Indian couple on the train who invited us to have dinner with them at their home in Benguela. I remember delicious corn chowder, and I still have the recipes she wrote out for me so I could try to duplicate the cuisine at home in Luanda. I've often wondered if I would invite complete strangers in for food. Probably not.

Maria Natalia helped care for Chris after we returned from home leave with our adopted five-week-old baby boy. She often told me she would probably never marry and have children, and he was as close as she would come to having her own child. She has followed his life as closely as she could from Portugal where all her family returned after Angolan independence. She came to Lisbon to stay with us for a few days when we lived there, and we were able to spend time with her and her sister when we visited Portugal a few years ago. I'm still trying to get her to visit us in the states, but she doesn't like to travel. She has a lovely, close-knit family. We were very fortunate to have her in our lives when we were young and so inexperienced.

After returning to the *metropole* (Portugal proper) and with only a fourth grade education, she worked her way up the bureaucratic government ladder. She held an important position in the public transportation sector of northern Portugal. Her sister told me she ran all the buses. She is a strong woman that one. She might have weighed all of 100 pounds soaking wet.

When we returned from home leave that year of 1967, we were armed with Similac and 18 cases of baby food for little Chris. That's the only time he ate green vegetables; he loved spinach. He led a princely life in Luanda. He walked from one end of the "spaceship" house to the other at nine months of age and figured how to unlock doors with the keys in them at about the same time. He was always very busy figuring out how things worked, what went together, how to take it apart and every once in awhile how to put it back together. He got used to everybody wanting to caress his fine golden hair.

Some of the $1,000 worth of groceries and paper products we had shipped to Angola on our transfer from Brasilia were still in the storage room when it was time to celebrate his first birthday. Some of the food was still edible after a year and a half. Unfortunately, the cake mixes didn't survive a long shelf life in tropical heat. Therefore, Maria Natalia and I started from scratch and conjured up two cakes— one a run-of-the-mill plain cake, full of eggs, so I guess it was a yellow cake, and the other chocolate.

There were probably eight American families in Luanda—four with the American Consulate and four drilling for oil with Gulf Oil (now Chevron) and Petro-Angola either in Cabinda or off-shore. All the kids were invited to the party as well as their moms along with the South African kids across the street with their mom, Marie, a good friend.

Now, I can laugh when I think about that party. It has all been caught on an 8mm movie, so I'm not exaggerating as I recount the afternoon. Picture this: Moms bring their shiny, spiffy kids to our lovely patio underneath the house surrounded by tropical vegetation. We often entertained with cocktail parties and dinners under the house rather than in the upstairs 'spaceship.'

The mothers made themselves comfortable sitting along one side of the patio to watch the proceedings while they enjoyed their delicate finger sandwiches and sipped tea from china cups. Maria Natalia and I took care of all the rest. Shepherding kids was no easy task as they ranged in age from one year (our birthday boy) to about six.

Chris, our honored guest perched in his high chair and scrutinized all that took place. I played games like pin-the-tail-on the donkey with the invited kid guests. The other moms sat smiling, perhaps waiting for me to topple over while masked. Chris watched in amazement. He hadn't witnessed this kind of behavior from his mother before.

Chris was dressed up in the blue two-piece outfit given to him by my longtime Scottish pen pal, Margaret. It was a special little suit, and as I was unsure as to how to launder it, I had saved it for this special day.

The chocolate cake left its mark all over Chris' face and didn't miss any part of his new suit either. He thoroughly enjoyed eating pieces of both cakes with both hands. He still ingests sugar as quickly as he can even in his 40s.

Being a new mother always striving for perfection, I got him cleaned up after the cake tasting. This time he was outfitted in one of his 'ducky' suits—appliquéd ducks on striped pastel-colored cotton fabric. His Grandmother Lore fell in love with a two-piece boy's outfit and proceeded to buy every size and color for shipment to Angola. She sent Chris a suit in each color—blue, green and yellow—in sizes six, nine and 12 months. He had nine duck suits. Today, he wore the blue 12-month sized duck suit. We all liked ducks.

Then, down on the ground he went. Instead of socializing, he made a beeline for the ramp path to the upper story and spent several minutes celebrating his birthday dallying among the dahlias. What a kid! To this day he continues to know where he's going and how to get there.

When it was time to leave, we left some good friends in Angola— missionary friends out in the hinterland and Angolans living in Luanda proper not to mention the Americans in the Consulate. We kept in touch with many of them over the years. We left Angola in late 1969 when Chris was 18 months old and returned to the States.

How's Your Liver?

Conversation for women at dinner or cocktail parties during this time was often about *criadas* (maids), *criancas* (children) and *doencas* (illnesses). These were the three main topics of conversation in the Portuguese-speaking world of which I was a part for a number of years. I think working women for the most part find their identities revolve around what they do at least eight hours a day for remuneration.

My 'productive' life took a different turn after marriage. I will admit that I clung mightily to my work as my identity before marriage. Involved in clinical cancer chemotherapy research after college graduation, I felt we were on our way to discovering treatments for cancer. The chase for cures continues. I didn't identify so much with my job in the Senate Democratic Policy Committee, because it didn't last long.

My identity changed; I was now referred to as a 'dependent' spouse. Fortunately, we were given the same language training as our United States government (USG) employed husbands. At least in Portuguese, we learned how to greet people properly, to order food, to inquire about lost luggage and to speak about additional mundane matters.

After attaining some proficiency, we were involved in conversations about the idiosyncrasies of the local people, their slang phrases and current political and economic developments. Although I was always more interested in people and culture, I did learn a thing or two about the economy and political situations in the Portuguese-speaking countries where we lived. Along with the USG employees, we read current events in the newspapers and discussed the contents.

Whenever we were involved in dinner or cocktail parties, we spoke Portuguese. Usually, conversations revolved around travel, the latest movies and the best restaurants. Both men and women participated. When the talk morphed into politics and who was up or who was down, the women separated themselves from the men to talk about the distaff side of life. The native Portuguese speakers always took the lead. Perhaps they didn't like economics or politics, so they channeled the discussion into *criadas, criancas and doencas* and moved away from the men, often to a different location. For the most part, these women were married to high-ranking government officials or military officers.

If you didn't have children, you participated in the *criadas* (maids) conversation. By the way, that word *criada* which I didn't use, meant that the maids were child-like in everybody's eyes and had to be taught. Note the common root for *crianca* and *criada.* Everybody had maids. So, they discussed them—what they did, what they didn't do, what they should do, *ad nauseum.*

Doencas (illnesses) were the second most important things to discuss. A fixation on the *figado* (liver) meant that I learned more about liver's functions than I ever cared to know. Why does a whole culture focus on one body part? All illnesses were blamed on the poor liver. Perhaps since digestive problems were rampant, the liver was blamed for the whole lot of possible infirmities.

Then, came the kids *(criancas).* Stay-at-home moms had both maids and kids to raise. If you spend all day every day with children, that's pretty much what you talk about with others. That's natural. Moms still do it today. Dads do it less unless they are house husbands which is way more common today than it was a few decades ago.

Think about it. The people serving us food this whole time spoke Portuguese. I wonder what they thought about our chatter. They were the *criadas* being discussed. How sad.

I know topics of conversation have changed in the ensuing years.

119

More women are out of the house and into the work force all over the world. Modern communication systems, if nothing else, have opened the world and its people to one another. E-mail alone would make it possible to chat with a friend elsewhere on the planet and then talk about that conversation at a dinner party. Then again, maybe the stay-at-home moms are discussing their exchanges with those expert computer guys in Mumbai. Discussing Mumbai computer experts' knowledge may boggle the mind, but it beats focusing on everybody's liver.

Taking Off

Our trip from Angola back to the States began somewhat awkwardly. Our plane didn't fly as scheduled.

It seems everybody we'd ever known in Luanda was at the airport to see us off. I often wondered what that meant. Were they glad to see us leave? Were they sorry? In any case our friends arrived with armloads of roses! They presented them to me to carry on the plane. I'd not seen that custom at work before. Flowers were offered when queens or first ladies descended from planes on arrival, but for Foreign Service families leaving? Here we were with our 18-month-old Christopher and the loot that entailed only to be handed many bouquets of flowers.

We said our tearful goodbyes and hopped on the plane for a direct flight to Johannesburg. I thought I'd never set foot in Luanda again. That made me very sad, because to this point, it was by far my favorite assignment. The plane almost took off. It came to a screeching halt just before it might have gone air born. Slowly, the plane retraced its steps back to the gate. We were told there were mechanical problems, but we'd already figured that out. We were asked to de-plane, and we found ourselves facing about half the friends who had come to see us off. I guess the other half had more faith that we would, in fact, leave. Or they thought, "Good riddance!" and headed for home. Anyhow, I returned before I thought I would!

Eventually, the plane was fixed, and with some trepidation, Mark, little Chris and I got back onto the aircraft. This time it left. The roses carefully placed in the overhead bin for the first 'departure' were droopier. Angola gets rather warm although it may not get as hot as Lagos, Nigeria, which can be an inferno at times. The flowers didn't live long enough to be put into vases. But, they served their purpose. It was a lovely sendoff.

The plane not ascending wasn't the most traumatic part of the trip if you can believe that. When we landed in Johannesburg, we were sprayed with DDT. I guess we were thought to be carrying a dangerous disease from Angola to South Africa. Perhaps we should have expected this since the three of us had been sprayed once before in Southwest Africa, now known as Namibia. That country was controlled by South Africa beginning in 1920 due to a mandate from the League of Nations after World War I. German-speaking people dressed in the clothing of the beginning of the 20th century were everywhere, so we had treated the country as a tourist destination and had made a short trip there to survey the situation. The South Africans must have had lots of DDT to spare using it in South West Africa as well. We survived.

In Jan Smuts Airport, we ran into friends—the only two people whom we knew in South Africa at that time. They didn't know we would be transiting their turf on our way to Mozambique. Can you imagine that? They were both in the airport when we walked from one gate to the next. Small world, eh? It was a joy to see Clare and Bob— who were living in Pretoria. They were among the first people we had met in the Foreign Service back in Rio de Janeiro. They happened to be meeting a flight from the States.

Our next plane took off without a hitch. Mark was assigned to do some investigating of the war between the Portuguese and the people of Mozambique. Chris and I stayed with the Martins in Lourenco Marques. That city has a new name since independence and is now called Maputo. It was fun to meet up with the Martins again—this time in Africa. Now I could explain what a *bidet* was to anyone who didn't know. Lolly and Tom had three children now. Little Susan was about Chris' age. Year and a half old kids don't play together much, however. They took turns poking one another in the tummy—

probably aiming at belly buttons.

Chris and I went for long walks around town. I remember eating a very popular Portuguese dish of clams and rice and going out for fabulous shrimp when Mark returned from the 'war.'

Now, after one more stop, we would be on our way to America! We visited Rabat and Casablanca on our way home, because we knew "we would never be assigned to Morocco." Men stared at us from behind curtains in hotel windows when we went walking about with Chris in his stroller. Had they never seen this kind of baby carriage before? I thought those men were creepy, but the food was fantastic. Yes, we did return to North Africa—the Foreign Service is full of surprises.

After our week long Moroccan sojourn, we flew to Chicago. All I remember about that trip to Illinois was that Chris identified all vehicles which looked like trucks and shouted out "Truck!" between O'Hare and Naperville where we visited the family. Come to think about it, trucks may have been new to him coming from Luanda. He also carefully looked at all his grandmother's 'pretties' on her corner cupboard shelves. He kept his hands in his pockets and used his eyes only. What a kid!

Home Again

So, there we were beginning our three-year stint in the States after three overseas assignments in the space of 18 months. We were able to stay in Angola for two years with a home leave in the middle.

I won't go into all our state side accomplishments right now—you'd get tired hearing them all. The big events were that Mark got the equivalent of a bachelor's degree in economics in an accelerated six-month course in the Department of State. The biggest event was Camille Susanne's birth two weeks before Christmas in 1970 whom we adopted the following March. Chris invited the Methodist minister to try some of 'Daddy's juice.' He also painted the red brick patio white one Sunday morning while Mark and I were engrossed in the Washington Post. I took driving lessons and learned to drive well, except the instructor skipped the part about merging onto highways. He might have been too frightened at the prospect. I still don't merge. Rest assured, I stay off highways.

We moved three times and ended up on Windsor Avenue in Alexandria where we bought a square brick house with a down payment from Mom and Dad. We needed three bedrooms, because we now had Camille. We now had the perfect family—a dad, a boy, a girl and a harried mom. Camille cooed and smiled all the time. Chris loved being the entertainment for his little sister.

Life was so different from Angola. To show you how different, let me tell you about Camille's first birthday. You'll recall all the details about Chris' party in Luanda—kids, mothers sipping tea, two cakes, dirty faces, etc.

It's December 11, 1971. We're back in the real world. We're living in our first home with a mortgage, and it's our second child's birthday. Camille Susanne was about to celebrate her first birthday. Without maids, fanfare, or gardens full of meter-high dahlias, we did the best we could with what we had. And, this time, we had a cake mix!

The kids had already been photographed in their Christmas finery in front of the felt Christmas tree advent calendar Grandma Brian had made them. So, Camille wasn't dressed in a fancy frock for her birthday picture. Because she was born two weeks before Christmas, more often than not, Camille's birthday pictures often show Christmas is coming as well as a little girl growing up.

The birthday photo shows Camille in an everyday dress, smiling for the camera, slapping her high chair table top, happy with the world! We weren't as flush as we felt we were in Africa where the cost of living was so much lower. We did have all we needed for a happy life—two great kids, a square brick house with three bedrooms, one bathroom, a fenced yard and a working sump pump in the basement.

Camille's first birthday cake was not only made from a cake mix, but there was the new recipe for boxed cakes in the land. The recipe called for four eggs, oil and dry pudding added to the dry ingredients in the box. It was so new that this was the first generation (one might say) on my part, and I could hardly wait to try it. Unfortunately, the camera doesn't lie.

We did photograph the birthday girl in her high chair in our charming 'colonial' dining room sitting beside our Brazilian table and in front of the hutch purchased for $10 before we were married, still antiqued green. Unfortunately, photographic evidence clearly shows a monumental lack of self-control on Baby Camille's mother's part.

There's a slice of cake missing. The camera does not lie. I'm thinking before I leave my earthly realm, I might ask a friend to 'photo shop' the cake so people won't wonder decades from now whether or not little Camille's mother got the 'mother of the year' award that year for sampling the cake—not just any cake—her daughter's first birthday cake—before the birthday girl had a chance to blow out the one candle. I live with the guilt.

Of course, Camille survived this indelicate behavior on the part of her mom. But, I've had to live with all those photos showing the missing piece for almost 40 years. Gluttony! Is that one of those seven deadly sins?

While studying French at the Foreign Service Institute for our impending assignment to Morocco (yes, Morocco!), I got the bug to work for George McGovern who was running for President. A paid position helped with childcare costs and transportation expenses between Alexandria and Washington, D.C. Unfortunately, our babysitter left me in the lurch by calling on a Sunday evening to inform me I was nuts to work for McGovern. Mom and Dad, also big McGovern supporters, told me to bring the kids to them so I could finish working at the national headquarters until after the election. I would never be able to repay that six-week babysitting debt. However, they were delighted to get in some extra innings with their Foreign Service grandchildren.

In September, 1972, Mark left for his assignment in Rabat. After the disastrous election and Thanksgiving dinner with the Illinois family, the kids and I followed him to Morocco. It took 20 hours to make the trip from Chicago to Boston to Paris and onto Rabat. I don't believe I ever did adjust to that country. It was by far the most 'foreign' we ever lived in.

Moving Slowly to Morocco

First we lived just under Africa's "hump." Now we lived way up at the northwestern part of the continent in a very different environment. Morocco is a wonderful country to visit as a tourist. In Brasilia we went without a few regular, normal, everyday creature comforts. Angola was remote and isolated with a war going on just outside town. In Morocco I never became comfortable with the culture. I will admit that it was my problem not Morocco's. French language training took place in Washington, DC unlike Portuguese language training in Rio de Janiero. I had interrupted my French studies by going to work for McGovern, so I spent most of the tour taking lessons in the Embassy a couple times a week.

Our two years in Rabat were filled with more adventures. The kids were young—Chris continued kindergarten there and Camille had a life of leisure behind the tall walls of the garden surrounding the villa where we lived.

Camille, when almost three, spoke Arabic like a Moroccan kid. We were very proud of her. We knew one word in Arabic—*Insallah* (god willing). Camille picked up the language from the kids who walked by our yard on their way to and from the *lyceu* (high school). The only problem with Camille's Arabic was the vocabulary. Evidently those privileged, upstanding Moroccan kids taught her filthy language— perhaps a drunken sailor's vocabulary. We learned that when she was returned home quickly from a play date with a little American girl the same age whose maid was offended at Camille's 'mouth!' There is a good side to this story and Camille's facility with languages. Her Arabic-speaking muscles were formed at an early age, and while in high school in Portugal, she learned from her Iraqi girlfriends that she spoke Arabic without a foreign accent. She has now forgotten all the Arabic words—the good and the bad.

Chris had a best friend around the corner from our house. Arthur was the son of an Embassy employee, exactly the same age as Chris and the only other boy in his classroom. Did they have fun? Fun is an understatement. Open classrooms were the rage in the Moroccan American school in those years, so nobody required that Arthur and Chris do any of the usual work. Instead, they built sculptures. Incredible sculptures. However, they didn't learn too much about reading, writing and arithmetic. We found that out at the next post. Chris caught up in second grade. I hope Arthur did too.

There was another American school at the Kenitra Navy Base. We were told the King's nieces and nephews attended that school. Of course, a chauffer-driven limo delivered them the 25 miles to the school each day. On arrival, a butler with a silver platter held high above his head carried their lunches into the school. Lunches were packed inside the Mickey Mouse lunch boxes purchased at the Kenitra PX. The King's family got first dibs on American stuff in that facility. Imagine, Mickey Mouse on a silver tray!

A couple of aging ragtag hippies, former McGovern workers, showed up in Rabat uninvited at one point to spend a week. I fed them, but they stayed in a small hotel in the medina. They were touring Africa picking fruit and posing nude for artists. They might have posed nude for folks other than artists, I thought. Without free room and board, they decided to head south to peddle their wares such as they were. That's a rather short, uninteresting tale, isn't it?

About this time, we had a robbery. While we were off on an extended weekend trip, a young Moroccan man forced himself into the house and found lots of stuff to swipe. The thief helped himself to some costume jewelry which had been willed to me by great Aunt Cora stored on the shelf in the bedroom wardrobe. He also heisted lace tablecloths, Moroccan rugs, booze and a small reel to reel tape recorder which Dad had given us for making talking tapes to send back home.

The robber loaded up the loot to store outside in a field until he could return for it. During his activity, he also downed a substantial amount of *Dubonnet*—showing his French colonial heritage. He left a mess. He was a very untidy robber. He evidently had seen a recent Egyptian film about jewels being hidden in frozen food packages in freezers. Yes, he opened the refrigerator's freezer door and tore apart the frozen vegetable boxes to look for jewels. He didn't bother to close the freezer door when he didn't find any. The ice cream drooled out the kitchen and down the marble steps to the foyer.

Imagine the surprised faces of the Embassy personnel when they discovered the break in! Ice cream slobbered down the steps. Moroccan employees in the embassy surmised Kadisha our maid had announced a weekend off, and the would-be robber heard which house would be empty. Kadisha lived with extended family and wore all the clothes she owned when she came to work. She needed to make sure they were still hers when her workday was over.

So, while we basked away in the sun at Club Med on the Mediterranean, someone was helping himself to our stuff—maybe even a relative of Kadisha's. Unusual as it was for a Moroccan woman, she smoked cigarettes and drank alcohol. She had a tough time staying sane during Ramadan, their month of fasting. She spent most of each day making *harira* (the soup with which they broke the fast each evening at sundown) and sneaking out into the back yard to the laundry tubs where nobody would look for her. There she smoked and drank. The Embassy suggested we let her go after the robbery. So, we looked for another maid.

To make matters worse, the police sold all our things although Mark had identified the objects as being ours. Once in awhile I think that perhaps a Moroccan lady is enjoying Aunt Cora's jewelry.

We made another memorable trip during our time in Morocco. Over Easter vacation one year we packed up and went to Spain—first by car to Tangiers where we caught a ferry to cross the Straits of

Gibraltar and then by car again as we toured around the southern part of the country.

Chris and Camille had a glorious time going from one playground to the next often with a boat ride in between. What we noticed early on was how shabby their clothes looked compared to Spanish kids' clothing. It was Easter after all. So, we bought them navy blue cardigan sweaters and what we dubbed 'Spanish jeans' made of very strong twill cotton. Chris' jeans and sweater got passed onto Camille when he outgrew them, and Camille passed both hers and his onto other smaller kids. Keep in mind if you need to buy jeans, Spain is the place.

More memorable than the tough jeans, however, is Camille's welcome to the ferry boat entering the harbor to carry us back home to Morocco. In her loudest three-year-old voice, she shouted to the waiting crowd, "Here comes the African Vagina!" She couldn't read yet—it was really the African Regina. A few English speakers smiled. I wondered where she had heard that word.

Back to the saga of the maids; after we let Kadisha go, we hired fastidious Fatima. I thought she would have a stroke one day when grape jelly jar fell out of the refrigerator splattering onto her newly scrubbed kitchen floor. She spoke no French, but I got the drift of how she felt about the jellied floor. She took Chris, then in first grade, home with her one weekend. She returned on Monday morning with our boy child in tow dressed like a little Moroccan kid in a striped blue tunic, white crocheted cap and pointed yellow slippers. His blue eyes and blond hair gave him away as a foreigner, however. He was treated like royalty at her home with leg of lamb, couscous and pigeon pie. I wonder if he would eat any of those foods today.

At one point in our tour, an Embassy officer traveled to Tunis. We asked if he had space to bring us back a bird cage. I'd never seen such intricate filigree work until I'd seen several from Tunisia. They were exquisite works of art, painted white with blue accents. He dutifully brought us back one which hung above our balcony outside the front living room. We purchased a bird at the outdoor market, and with much fanfare, said bird was placed in the cage with requisite water and food. During the night, he hung himself on some of that beautiful filigree. So much for beautiful cages—the bird would have had a longer life in his cardboard box in the market.

Soon after that sad event, Mark and I traveled to the Sahara and the high Atlas mountains of Morocco. Vendors along the road were selling delicious blue colored stones. We had never before encountered rocks like this. Mind you, I was only 32 so hadn't seen all the blue stuff in the universe yet.

With much cajoling and pleading on my part to buy another decoration for the patio, Mark finally stopped the car. We chose a big perfect rock. Mark, once again, gave in to my whim and plucked over the $25 in equivalent dirham (the Moroccan currency). This rock was put onto the same balcony taking the place of the Tunisian bird cage. The rock would not commit suicide. You know what? The rock didn't make it through the first night either. Rain washed the blue color right off it. Moral: Beware of cobalt blue rocks when traveling in the Atlas Mountains, and always check birdcages for suicide potential.

Should you find yourself in Morocco on winding roads under construction or rehab of some kind, you won't have to read Arabic to know the ropes. You will be stopped from proceeding ahead by a live person using the universal arm gesture for 'Stop.' You will sit there wondering how long it will take before you can go ahead. You will note that the last car coming from the opposite direction in the single open lane will have a tree branch in hand which is handed to the flagman to signal that the traffic flow should reverse. Two-way radios are not needed at all—just a big branch.

Here's the last story of loss. Female problems were interfering with my life once again, so I made an appointment at the Kenitra Navy Base to see an American doctor. He was appalled at my emergency situation and ordered a plane to fly me to Rota, an American Naval base outside Cadiz, Spain for surgery. The time for a hysterectomy had arrived. A plane was found, Mark's secretary located my toothbrush and bathrobe and arrived at the naval base just as I was being loaded onto the plane.

To make a long story a bit shorter, Mark immediately found an

American neighbor to look after the children while he tried to make his way to Spain. Unfortunately, the King of Morocco was traveling in the Straits of Gibraltar, so Mark couldn't cross into Spain until the King was out of the way. (Security, you know). He arrived the next day just after the six hours of surgery ended. I was pain free from the moment I 'came to.' Problems had plagued me all my adult life, and now I would live without pain. I stayed in Rota for another month until they could find a pilot willing to fly 'an older American woman' back to Rabat.

Entertaining Muslims in our home was quite an experience. The men all drank Scotch, and before a party even began, they asked for 'pink chicken.' Strictly forbidden by their religion, they, nevertheless, loved eating ham at foreign diplomats' homes.

Many of the women I encountered, who unlike their husbands had not been educated in France, spoke only Arabic and arrived dressed to the nines in their intricately hand-embroidered, multicolored silk caftans. Then, they plunked themselves down on the sofas and proceeded to keep entertained talking between themselves in Arabic. I made myself useful by helping the waiters serve up the pink chicken!

The radio stations played only Arabic music—still dissonant to my ears, and the *muezzin* called people to prayer five times a day from a nearby mosque. All very foreign! It should have been fascinating. I'd surely love to give it another try now that I'm mature. Next time, I would make an attempt to learn some of the language—at least a couple of Camille's effective cusswords.

It was during our tour in Morocco when all my senses were assaulted and forced to run on overdrive. The Khemmisett souk, located some miles outside Rabat, has been up and running since the Middle Ages, and we were able to visit it once. I had been told it was both colorful and smelly and I could purchase anything from an abortion to a camel. I needed neither, but one Tuesday morning, we decided to have a look at this place.

That day, we had the equivalent of $75 in dirham, the Moroccan currency, plus a bit of change so we could fortify ourselves with mint tea, always minty and sweet. I remember we had that amount of money, because we made one purchase and emptied out Mark's wallet to pay for it.

Out in the middle of nowhere we came upon acres and acres of activity aka the Khemmisett souk. It looked like only the white, hive-shaped bread ovens were permanent fixtures. Tents and shacks and wagons looked to have been set up just for the market day. Mules and horses served as a backdrop. What a stage set it was.

The souk doesn't resemble your friendly local food store in any way. Chickpeas and beans are not sold in cans neatly stacked on shelves with prices clearly marked. They are instead available for purchase, uncooked, in bins, at whatever price the vendor thinks he can get you to pay. The lentils, peas and beans produced a beautiful tapestry of color, design and texture. Olives in infinite variety are displayed in the same way. I've never seen so many bins full of figs, almonds, couscous, dates and prunes. Also stored in huge baskets displayed in carts were marvelous spices—cinnamon, cloves, cumin, cardamom, saffron—as well as many exotic herbs and teas, which I've not seen or smelled since. Those were the good smells!

Moving right along from that fragrant, variegated scene, we saw fresh fish, pickled fish, dried fish, living eels, dead goats, not yet skinned dead lambs hanging from hooks, cows' heads, cows' other parts, live chickens, dead chickens, horses' heads, horses' other parts, big birds, little birds and on and on it went. If it ran, swam or flew, you could find it at the Khemmisett souk ready for purchase to be made into something delectable.

Old men sat along the sidelines smoking their hashish. All ages of folk were at various times seen drinking mint tea, a smell which permeated almost every corner of Morocco. A variety of bread freshly baked in outdoor wood-burning ovens was also free for the smelling and available for purchase.

In addition fresh fruits and vegetables were everywhere. Under those beautiful blue skies, tomatoes never looked so red or oranges so orange. Both rose and orange waters could be purchased to add a delicate intensity to a cookie or cake recipe.

The Moroccan equivalent of Williams Sonoma was situated in one special area. You could buy all the implements you might ever need for food preparation from *couscousieres* (special pots for cooking couscous) to earthenware *tagine* pots used to make stews like I'd never tasted before or since. Clothing in all sizes and shapes for fair weather or foul was being hawked. And, there were kids everywhere, tugging at you, begging for money or whatever else you might give them. We were always fending off little kids a dozen at a time. I think now they worked in packs.

We didn't hear anyone speaking French. The Berber language and Arabic rumbled along. It seemed everybody talked at once. Both languages are melodic and sounded dramatic to my ears. Along with the cacophony of languages were boom boxes, doing what they all do best—all over the world—invading your space with their sounds. All Moroccan music seemed to be written in a minor key. So, in addition to not being able to understand the lyrics, I don't think I ever heard anything more than once, so I could never 'name that tune' or hum one either.

Now, let's return to the $75 purchase. A man and his wife, at least two kids tagging along, and she, very pregnant, holding a relatively young baby, approached us. It was obvious they were either destitute or very good actors. We didn't need the rug they were hawking, but it was obviously hand made, unusual and six inches narrower at one end than the other which could be useful fitting into tight spaces. Most important, the family needed the money. The mother had indeed woven the rug on a home made loom. I don't remember how much they asked for it, but we showed them how much money we had, and they took it happily.

On this warm Tuesday morning, we slung the rather damp, scratchy, new multicolored wool rug with its special, unique odor over Mark's shoulders and off we marched to our car to load it up.

Since I began weaving a few years after leaving Morocco, I've often thought about the Moroccan lady with all those kids. How did she find the time to dye the yarn, weave the rug, care for children, bake bread, serve tea and still make the family's meal at the end of each day?

Of all the experiences we had in Morocco, this is the one which continues to stand out in our memories. Everything was in the Khemmisett souk. Other adventures might contain some of what we saw that day, but no other experience equaled the totality of this one. Looking back on our stroll through that Tuesday souk, I realize that we were able to touch, taste, feel, smell, see and hear what others going to that market had experienced hundreds of years before our arrival—except for the boom boxes, of course.

The terrain of this land is some of the most beautiful in the world. With a lovely long length of coastline, the Atlantic Ocean can be seen from much of the land. The mountains and desert give additional incredible views. Huge castle-like structures of sandstone dot the landscape. Inside are tiled walls, gold bath fixtures and opulence like I'd never before or since witnessed. Believe me, oases do exist! Indeed, when seeing tall date palms off in the distance, one can be sure a sanctuary of shade, water and dates is nearby. Mountains, valleys, seascapes—Morocco has it all.

We were invited for dinners in several Moroccan homes and were treated as well as guests can be treated. So, I'll chalk up my Morocco unhappiness to not understanding the culture well enough, not speaking Arabic and being sick most of the time. That's the story of my doing time in a Moroccan villa. I'd make a better job of it now.

Adapting!

Once accustomed to the gypsy Foreign Service life, moving every few years continued to be a challenge but turned into fun as well. Experienced diplomats told us to keep our family size to two kids so if someone yelled, "Yankee, go home," we could each tuck a kid under an arm and leave the other free to carry a suitcase. We were now a family of four moving. The nesting instinct was very strong with me as I always focused on our home—at least until we were settled in.

After leaving Morocco, the most foreign of all our assignments, we were transferred to Belgium. While almost assigned to Ghana, the Secretary of State, Henry Kissinger, determined people were becoming too specialized in particular areas of the world, so he shook things up, and we were sent helter skelter to different areas. Mark was labeled an "Africanist" although we had served in just two African posts—Angola, a Portuguese province, and Morocco in North Africa. He needed to be moved off the African continent to a different location.

Europe was in our future. Some Foreign Service personnel never left Europe. Officers were supposed to be available for world wide service, but many 'Europeanists' bit the bullet and stuck it out in Europe. Henry Kissinger changed that, too. The Europeanists had to find new territory to make room for folks like us 'Africanists.' We were assigned to Brussels.

This lovely city had its beginnings as a 10th-century fortress town. One can still see parts of the fortress wall even today. Now its population is about two million. The city is home to many international organizations, the Economic Union (EU), the North Atlantic Treat Organization (NATO), and numerous diplomats and public servants. Nineteen communes, some French-speaking and some Flemish or Dutch-speaking, comprise the city. Linguistic tensions are omnipresent. Along with food and rain, language was the third main dinner party conversation between Belgians and foreigners.

We arrived in Brussels rather late in the house-hunting season, so most of the available rental housing was taken. Since foreigners from around the world live there, they all need housing. It seemed like everyone had a place to live but us. We finally did find a cute little A-frame house just a short walk from the tram's last stop in Kraainem, a Flemish-speaking commune. The neighbors were friendly, our new American friends the Woods were a block away, and there was a Flemish/French-speaking school nearby for Camille to attend.

There was much touring to do in and around the city, not to mention nearby European countries, many which could be visited over a day's time or on a weekend. Although the dollar was low and everything was expensive, it was a plush posting for us. The low dollar didn't stop us from traveling and getting the most we could from this European posting. We thought it would be the only one.

The kids got somewhat weary of weekend travel to yet another cathedral and eating yet another picnic in the car if it was raining. However, ornate, century old churches provided something for everybody. Most had huge clocks with moving parts for our budding car guy, Chris, and Camille loved using the marble tomb markers of burial grounds in floors as stepping stones or for a solitaire game of hopscotch. Mark was mesmerized by both the architecture and great works of art. I could always sneak outside to smoke while the family was otherwise occupied.

During this four-year tour in Brussels, we watched all episodes of *Upstairs Downstairs*. By the time we got to Portugal, *Cheers* was our main TV entertainment from one week to the next. Limited English-language TV was a good thing then with two teens in the house.

Brussels was rewarding in so many ways. We were living where much European history had taken place. Rather than the kids having to wait to live in Europe during their junior years abroad, they could get a taste of it as pre-teens—the best of all possible times for family tourism.

Chocolate and coffee are two of the outstanding reasons to love Brussels. Incredibly beautiful ancient architecture was everywhere. Food was even better than French food. Public transportation was excellent. Flea and antique markets were everywhere. Because of the low dollar, when we ate out, we ate a pot of *moules* (mussels) and a pile of *frits* (French fries)—ample food for our family of four. I found everything about Brussels classy—even the *moules*.

My good friend Carol Wood introduced me to the *Group de l'amitie* (friendship group) which met on Thursday mornings each week. As far as I know, this activity was unique to Brussels. It should exist around the world.

The story was that a Belgian Ambassador's wife found people unfriendly in Luxembourg when her husband was assigned there. Luxembourg is so close to Brussels one could almost commute to work. In any case, she didn't feel welcomed by the country's people. She didn't want the foreigners living in Brussels feeling unwelcome, so she formed *groups de l'amitie'* throughout the city through the American Women's Club.

This woman had lots of friends—at least one in each of the 19 communes—and put them in charge of getting foreigners and Belgian women together to get to know one another. This activity surely had some rippling effects—at least in our group. In fact some 35 years later, we went touring around Ireland with Judy, a friend from this association.

These groups integrated us foreigners into the life and culture of the city. The Belgian women helped with language practice. Belgians could practice English, and the Americans and Brits could work on their French. When I first started attending, we played Scrabble—French and English together in the same game. (Of course it was confusing!)

Three women who became close friends and who later visited

us both in Portugal and the United States were Eva, Yvette, and the aforementioned Judy. The first meeting I attended was at Eva Gutmanns' apartment. She was a German-born Jew who managed to be on what may have been the last train out of Germany at the time of World War II. She worked as a domestic in Britain until the war ended. After becoming a naturalized American, she met her husband, Theo Gutmanns, a Latvian-born, United Nations linguist. Years later, they retired to Brussels.

Yvette, a Belgian woman at the first meeting, had recently been dumped by her husband. They had three children—all in their teens. Yvette was just turning 50 and had no means of income, so she painted walls and hung wallpaper for anybody who needed these services. I had seldom seen that kind of spunk, especially from women of her social standing. I have no idea what the divorce laws in Belgium are, but she didn't come out too well. Many others in the group suffered through their husbands' affairs, so the laws were probably not too pro-female.

Yvette and her brother were the owners of a large, rustic residence in Sibret. House poor would be an understatement. Located near the *Bois de Boulogne*, her ancestral home could have told some fantastic stories from several centuries. The Battle of the Bulge, fought over the winter months of 1944–1945, the last major Nazi offensive against the Allies in World War Two, took place near her home. When we visited, we saw various generations of furniture, linens and other necessities of a very privileged life. The house was the entire village and occupied its main square. Each year, Yvette invited the *group de l'amitie'* to spend the weekend closest to New Years. What a treat that was—to live in such a grand house once a year. Yes, with at least a dozen bedrooms, a couple dozen people slept in beds.

We discovered when we spent time near the *Bois de Boulogne,* people in cafes made themselves known to us and told us how much they loved the Americans, their liberators. Mark and I were children when our country was liberating Europe, but we were the recipients of their thanks. We were often very humbled to be representing the United States abroad.

Yvette visited us twice in the United States. During our time in Madison, Wisconsin, (an academic 10-month stint), we rented a turn-of-the-century, modest Victorian house. Unlike many other old houses in this college town, it had not been divided into apartments for students. Everyone asked, "Do you live in the whole house?" We found that such a strange question—we had three bedrooms and one bath—not out of line for an American family of four.

When Yvette visited, she talked about the cute little house we were living in. We all do look at things differently. Yvette visited us again in the 90s in Winchester, but she was beginning to show signs of dementia. At that point, she spoke only French and talked ad infinitum about all her friends who had suffered from cancer. She was very different from the old Yvette. This may have been her last trip alone. When she returned to Belgium and telephoned us, she talked on and on, repeating many things and then realized the cake in the oven was burning, so we hung up quickly. I've not heard from her since then. She was one of many who enriched our lives immeasurably.

Four years of weekly meetings over coffee made for a tight group of friends. Usually, 15-20 women attended each week. Of course, our language facilities improved, but more than that, we became a close community of several different nationalities. My mother visited once and remarked on how she had never seen such a diverse group of women intent on being so helpful to one another.

Our tour in this large European capital might have been very long and lonely. Instead, I left more friends there when we were assigned back to the states than in any other post. I hope these friendship groups still exist. Perhaps they have caught on in other sophisticated world capitals by now. It does make a large city feel like a village when you can make many friends and spend time with them each week. We were able to keep in touch with one another for about 20 years. Then, some of the older members passed away. I know of only two besides me who are left from my group from the mid-1970s. Those women enhanced my life in that big foreign city, and I will always be grateful for their friendship and kindnesses.

Let's return to the mid-career diplomat and his family and the nitty-gritty of our everyday living. Our A-frame house may have been charming, but it was too small. There was no way to carry out the entertaining required of Mark's job. We had one of those half sized refrigerators for our family of four. Chris slept in the attic which had been painted red, white and blue—cute but disastrous for his asthma. Camille had a little room which should have been a closet. What was to be the master bedroom had to serve as a family room, because the living room was so small. When Mark or I stood up in the bathtub, that darned sloped roof A hit you smack dab in the head. Several headaches resulted, believe me.

We talked with our landlady about the house being too small. It was a touchy subject since she and her husband had built the house and lived in it for 25 years. They had raised their two children in this space. There were many reasons they could do this, I suppose, but I didn't want to sacrifice our family's mental health to stay there four years. Mme. Morreau relented and promised if I could find her another renter and could pass the exit inspection, she would release us from the lease.

We've not run into this inspection business in any other post. Landlords everywhere else we lived were delighted to have American tenants backed up by an Embassy. Rental payments were assured. Embassy employees didn't destroy property. In Belgium it may have been a necessary law just because of the sheer number of foreigners and the enormous amount of rental housing in the city.

Called the *etat d'lieu* (state of the property), renters lived in mortal fear of being fined very large sums of money at the end of their leases if the property wasn't perfect—exactly as it was when they moved in. Photographs of all surfaces were taken when a lease was signed. When tenants left, the current state of the property was compared to the photographs. No allowances were made for wear and tear as is done here in the United States.

Being the daughter of an immaculate housekeeper gave me the confidence that I could leave any place better than I found it. In fact, when we left our second home in Brussels after the tour was over, the landlord telephoned me to say I had left the townhouse in much better shape than it was given to us. I was happy to receive that recognition from the man who could have fined us thousands dollars had the walls and floors not met the 'state of the property' photos. Spackling along with white toothpaste can cover up most holes and blend with white paint on walls.

Since I love looking at real estate, I had a new role. In no time at all, we found a fabulous townhouse on Avenue Capitaine Piret in the Woluwe-St. Pierre commune. I then went to work to find our landlady some new tenants. Because it was a charming house—straight out of a fairy tale book, I had no trouble finding a tenant. Someone else would fall in love with it. People from the Canadian Embassy came by on a sunny day when brownies were baking in the oven. What luck. They signed a nine-year lease.

Canadians are like us—it was too small for them too. Although couples without children moved in, I heard over the years, they moved out again rather quickly. They probably got tired of bumping their heads on the A-frame after baths. I felt sorry for the landlady, but she did have a lease, and she got paid each month whether or not anybody was living there.

The townhouse was perfect. The kids could now have a pet. Their first one was a guinea pig whom they named Henry Kissinger. It was their way of saying "thank you" for the assignment in Belgium. Geordie, the goofy dog, joined the household a bit later, and Henry moved to an Army base in Germany when we left Belgium. My brother Mike was stationed in Germany at the time, so we were able to see him and meet some of his friends quite often. One of his friends took Henry to the Army zoo to live out his life eating lettuce and looking cute. We hope he lived happily ever after, as they say, but when he left us, he didn't understand any German.

Both kids went to the Department of Defense (DOD) school, the only practical, English-speaking choice for Embassy families; there were other excellent English-language schools in Brussels, but Embassy families' educational allowances covered just the DOD school.

That is no longer the case. American kids whose parents are

142

assigned to one of the three embassies in Brussels (bi-lateral, EC and NATO) can attend any school these days. Other rules were changing in the Department of State also. No longer would spouses be judged on their free work for the US Government in efficiency reports. In my opinion, they should never have been part of the employees' efficiency reports. They were not employed, and they certainly were never paid for their labors (even if they did look at their efforts as careers).

Discussions of this new rule were fascinating. Many spouses wanted to be included in the efficiency reports. After all, they were doing the work for the government and wanted recognition for same. I never felt that way.

In my generation before young women settled down to marriage, children and domesticity, they could become nurses, teachers or secretaries. There were exceptions, of course, but for the most part, those were the career paths available to women. Most 'dependent' spouses in the Foreign Service at that time would fit into these career categories.

All my women friends at the beginning of our years in the Foreign Service happened to be teachers, nurses or secretaries. Some found work in embassies or in American schools. I found work whenever I wanted to work, because I could type. (Remember how Mom told me to learn to type so in case anything ever happened to my husband I could get a job? Thanks again, Mom!)

I don't remember that any of the spouses of Foreign Service personnel had other careers than the aforementioned ones during the first few years of our time in the Foreign Service with a couple of exceptions—artists. So, although most wives were college graduates and might have pursued careers, they were not doing so.

After the first ten years of our time in the Foreign Service, female spouses started showing up at post with careers other than the above three. A ballerina, a concert pianist and a lawyer arrived as 'dependent spouses' in the Embassy in Brussels. They had left their careers behind to follow their husbands. I don't know if they looked for work in Belgium or not. I always felt sorry for them—especially for the ballerina and concert pianist. Just think how many hours had been spent on practicing to become and then, rather than becoming, they fell in love and followed.

About this time, many more females became Foreign Service officers. At one time, if you had been an officer married to an officer, one of you would have to leave the Forcign Service to be a dependent spouse. Crazy world out there, wasn't it? Mostly, the women left. They could be reinstated years later at their old pay grades when the law changed. If an officer had a foreign-born spouse, they would have to return to the United States until she became a naturalized American citizen. I don't believe that is true any longer either. There's something not fair about that, too. Being a spouse isn't always so easy.

In Brussels, an artist brought along her paints; she rented a studio outside the home, painted and gave shows. That was a good lesson for some of the rest of us—we could become artists! I bought a Dutch loom and started to become a weaver in 1976.

Enough of a favorite hobby for now. Let's return to spouses, careers and the Foreign Service. By the mid-90s, spouses with careers were often not coming to posts at all. By then, many more women had joined the service, and their male spouses were staying home in the States—to practice medicine or law in the two cases I recall from our last posting in Brasilia.

These days with wars and terrorism, often the spouses and families of Foreign Service personnel aren't even allowed to accompany the employee to many parts of the world. Our Foreign Service has changed that much in four decades. It has gone from supportive female spouses going along with the husbands' careers and foregoing any they might have had by living abroad, to just staying in America and letting the working spouse go work wherever in the world that might be. Separated families surely don't feel so far away from one another with current technology connecting them. Nevertheless, they probably didn't sign on for a separated marriage. Hopefully, many are able to live at post and work on line from all over the world.

I'm grateful Mark's career began in 1965. In my case I wasn't determined to have a career. In many places in the world, you have more free time because of household help, you can volunteer and pursue many new activities, and in many places, you can spend the whole time touring. I grew to love the gypsy life after awhile. Experiencing new cultures, food, languages, making new friends and visiting different countries every three or four years isn't a bad way to enjoy the journey. Maybe those days are gone forever too. Two income families seem to be the rule rather than the exception these days.

Of course, many friends and family visited us in Brussels. We had more visitors there and in Portugal than at any other place we lived during our time in the Foreign Service.

Belgium was the perfect jumping off point for travel in Europe. We visited The Netherlands often, because it was so close by. Germany wasn't much further. Our vacations were usually in one place and one rented house. We spent a week in Brittany, another in the Lake Country of England, but the most memorable place for the kids was probably our Easter holiday in Provence.

Since Dad had been sick part of the time he and Mom had visited us in Brussels, he returned the following year for our spring holiday. Driving from Belgium to France was not without incident. We weren't yet out of the country when Camille from the back seat proclaimed, "That man in the front seat who is not a member of our family is giving me a headache." She could have been slightly more diplomatic since he was actually the family patriarch. The lit cigar was the culprit. Dad tried not to smoke in the car from then on, but it wasn't easy, and he got grouchy.

We spent a delightful week in a stone house in the middle of a vineyard for as far as one could see. Dad was ecstatic with the Roman ruins in Orange while Chris and Camille made up new rhymes about the bridge in Avignon. Lyrics about the 'palace of the poops' and other body functions were put to song. I'll bet they could come up with the words today as they repeated them so many hundreds of times.

I had a terrible time leaving Belgium—as I did leaving all posts— except for Morocco. I went around to all the shop owners to tell them how much I had appreciated their good service and how I would miss them—the baker, the butcher, the mom and pop general store.

145

There, at my favorite general store, I broke down completely but left giving the owner lots of good advice on how wonderful it is to have a hysterectomy which she was facing. All in French. Hope she didn't die or anything.

I said goodbye also to all the merchants with whom I dealt in Lisbon. One of them responded, "It's good you are going back to your own people where you belong." That was from the lady in the feed and seed store behind our garden wall. I think she meant well.

I don't mean to be ungrateful at having to spend most of my adult life 'on holiday.' At times, I'm sorry I didn't pursue a career (even though some wives thought being the spouse was the career). I can think of so many things I wouldn't have become. I might have been like our niece Tricia's little girl Raeanna who recently told her mom, "I'm moving to Hollywood!" When her mother asked why, she responded, "So I can get into the Guinness Book of World Records." She just hasn't decided which record to pursue. This is the same child who told her mom to buy a mousetrap on St. Patrick's Day so they could catch a leprechaun. Her world record will involve creativity for certain! She lives in a time when she can become anything she would want to be. And, she doesn't have to live in Hollywood.

Back to Reality

When we left Belgium, I thought I was leaving Europe forever. What a summer we had! Mark was about to embark on a masters degree in economics at the University of Wisconsin at Madison. He spent the summer in Washington, DC, doing preparatory work in economics and calculus to ready him for the rigors of graduate work. He was turning 40 and would be in classes with kids half his age.

Chris, Camille and I spent the summer at Mom and Dad's home in Illinois. I shudder to think about that now. Company after three days exhausts me—I seem to run out of both food and energy. Anyhow, there we were. Of course, with Chris and Camille and their two cousins, Tricia and David, living in the same town, the summer was not uneventful. We took Geordie with us. You'll learn more about Geordie when I tell you about all the pets we've loved over the years.

This was the summer the kids took swimming lessons at the Naperville pool. One afternoon, Chris bulleted too fast from the pool to the parking lot where we waited to drive home. Unfortunately, he forgot to watch where he was going and dashed neck first into a wire protecting flower beds. It hurled him to the cement pavement and almost knocked him out. He spent a week in the hospital with a concussion. The doctor thought his head X-rays looked as if he had been in a motorcycle accident. After a week's worth of ice cream and Jell-O, he was well again. Grandma Brian bestowed him with a new nickname, 'Fleet Foot.'

Thankfully, Chris recovered completely, and we moved to Wisconsin. We felt very fortunate to be living there for an academic year. We would be close to family members. Unfortunately, my dad had a stroke in early November, but, on the other hand, we were close by and could visit Naperville often. Mark studied all the time it seems, but we did have quality time with him each weekend.

The State Department shipped all our worldly possessions from Belgium and the storage warehouse onto Madison. Again, our biggest problem was finding a place to live late in the summer when all rental properties were taken. At one point Mark was given a phone number from Student Housing and realized he was talking with the Governor's wife about using their lake home which was available to rent for the year. She said, "The election looks good, but…" It was that uncertainty which kept cautious Mark from signing on. The Governor just might not win the upcoming election, and in that case, he and his family would need the house since they'd be moved out of the mansion. We didn't want to take a chance on having to vacate property (probably in snow) before the year was up. We found a pleasant Victorian house, modestly renovated. They forgot to put insulation in the kitchen, so I baked Christmas cookies wearing fur-lined boots and long underwear because it was rather chilly.

We had many visits from family and thoroughly enjoyed our time living in the Midwest. I studied weaving and fiber arts the whole year and learned a great deal from the master weaver, my professor, Joyce Marques Carey.

Other highlights of the Madison year were building a playhouse in the driveway from a moving crate (larger than some student housing), Chris' and Camille's reading *The Hobbit* with their Chinese studying babysitter Dan while sitting in a tree, ice skating on the lake, camping in tents while a tornado raged outside, climbing through mounds of snow to watch Russian athletes play hockey on New Year's Eve, bussing back and forth to Illinois on weekends and surviving the long winter and its snow—all in ten months. Oh, yes, Mark did earn his masters degree in economics, the reason we were all there in the first place.

A final highlight occurred on my 40th birthday. You can imagine when the snow piled up, it stayed frozen and lasted until late spring. Camille just kept climbing over taller and taller mountains of the stuff when she walked to third grade down Johnson Street. Mark rode his bike at times—Wisconsinites know how to keep snow shoveled month after month. There's no trick to this: If you don't shovel, you get fined.

My birthday arrived as it always had in early April, and Christopher told me he was too sick to attend school that day. He hadn't appeared ill the night before. Since I was naturally suspicious, I told him if he did stay home, he'd have to stay in his room and in bed. He couldn't be well miraculously ten minutes after school began. He was earning all A's, so he wasn't feigning illness to escape classes—as far as I could tell.

I carried on as usual that day with no classes of my own at the University. I must have treated myself to a nap.

After dinner that night, Chris produced a white box with six inch high red numbers, $4.12 written on the top. Inside was a birthday cake. Astonished, I asked, "What's this?"

He responded with, "Mom, nobody ever bakes you a cake." He had stayed home from school ostensibly for this surprise. Sneaking downstairs to the dirt-floored basement to get his bike, he took it out through the basement door and rode six blocks to the Eagle store to purchase a cake using every bit of money he had. As far as I was concerned, he did nothing wrong for the next 25 years!

During spring break, I made a quick trip to Virginia to find us a house to live in. It was waiting for us after the school year was over, and we moved right in—more or less ready to try the suburban lifestyle outside Washington, DC. None of us was crazy about living in a cul-de-sac with 14 other kids, so we moved to Clifton after a couple of years. There, we were all happy again!

Back to Europe! Hurrah!

We left the Portuguese-speaking world when we departed Luanda, Angola, in 1968, and now we were back. This time, we'd get to know the *metropole* (metropolis)—the word people from the Portuguese homeland used while living in one of its provinces. In 1983 Mark was assigned to Lisbon as the economic counselor, and away we went!

Since our ten months in Madison, Wisconsin, we had lived in an enormous suburban sprawl in Fairfax, Virginia. Becoming bored with our cul-de-sac living, we moved to the outskirts of Fairfax County just outside the hamlet of Clifton. The kids enjoyed life there too—surrounded by country. We were all excited about moving to Portugal, however.

We quickly learned after our arrival in Lisbon that many families in the Embassy had children about the same ages as ours, so finding friends was easy. I might add it was comfortable for us parents too—we almost always knew the families of Chris and Camille's friends, and we were all able to keep tabs on them. They say you shouldn't move two year olds or teenagers, but we got lucky.

Our assigned house was waiting for our arrival. We were going to live in Estoril, a suburb of Lisbon situated near both the train line and the ocean. It was built as a party house; the servants had stayed and guarded it during the time when a communist-influenced military government was in control of the country. For this, the servants had a de-facto claim on the house. We had a maid (of sorts) and a gardener (of fewer sorts) waiting for us when we arrived. They lived beneath the house in their own apartment. They served our predecessors tolerably well, but our relationship wasn't so good.

We stayed in the house for about a year after which time we found a much more suitable place for our family. This next dwelling was ancient and had even survived the 1755 earthquake and fire which Lisbon suffered. Once it served as a brothel for fishermen. The mayor of Cascais lived there one time. The deposed King of Italy celebrated birthdays in the home when it was inhabited by some of his friends; there was said to have been a Renoir hanging in the dining room. Charming is an understatement; the house actually meandered around a corner on *Navegantes* Street (named thus in honor of the Portuguese explorers). The whole family appreciated living there—at least until near the end of our tour when drug dealers and their customers began to get noisy in the bar across the street.

The dogs enjoyed a white-washed walled-in garden with the largest palm tree of the village. The French doors of the dining and living rooms opened to the garden beyond. Tile-clad window seats were situated at every street side window so in other eras young women could talk to the young men outdoors but stay safe inside their homes. Old worldly, isn't it? Our family didn't bother with such vestigial remains but used the seats to hold plants most of the time. The house wrapped around a corner, and it was easy to describe to anyone where we lived because the dwelling was so unique.

Portugal was the best family post in the Foreign Service for us. Mark and I were able to renew friendships with Angolans and Portuguese whom we had known earlier in Angola. We arrived at post with the Portuguese language under our belts. Well, almost.

Days after arriving, Chris, Camille and I walked over to a bistro/ café where umbrella topped tables sprawled down the lawn in front of the establishment looking out to the sea. I thought we needed a break from unpacking, so away we went. I was attempting to teach them a few Portuguese words at the time. I guess I should have checked out the dictionary before sallying forth. I ordered each of us a *laranjeira* instead of *suco de laranja*. The waiter just grinned. I had ordered us each an orange tree instead of orange juice. He smiled and chirped in English, "We'd all like to have our own orange tree!" The lesson: Refresh the language a bit before ordering drink or food—especially in front of the kids.

We knew when Mark accepted the four-year assignment in Lisbon as the Embassy's Economic Counselor that Chris would have to leave for college before the end of the tour while the rest of us remained in Portugal. Worse than that, Camille would have to leave to return for her senior year of high school in the States. That must be about the worst thing a parent can do to a teen—send him/her to a new school for the final year. By the senior year friends and cliques are well established. Camille rallied and managed to do well in her studies partially because the carrot we held out was a trip back to Lisbon for the graduation of her American School of Lisbon class. She graduated from James Madison High School in Vienna, Virginia, one day and left for a two-week trip to Portugal the next. She was able to attend her class' graduation.

We learned from Chris after his first year in college at Pittsburg State University in Kansas that during his first semester he would sit his car and cry from homesickness. His fellow students didn't understand why his parents lived in Portugal since he wasn't Portuguese. At least he had grandparents in northern Illinois whom he could visit on school breaks and during Thanksgiving. I learned from the memorial service held for my parents in 2009 that Mom baked and sent him cookies while he was in college. Nobody ever told me.

Despite these unfortunate situations, we all loved our time in Portugal. Two blocks from the ocean, our 18th century house afforded us a perfect location for mom and pop groceries and fresh produce, for reasonably priced restaurants and for quick access to the train ride into the city or to one of the other suburbs along the line.

The school bus stop was a short two-block walk away. So were the bars. Unfortunately, if you were tall enough to reach the bar, liquor was easily accessible. We dealt with that—more or less. On our way to a weekend camping trip in the Algarve, we stopped along the way for lunch at which time Mark asked the kids what kind of beer they'd like to have with their food. We knew they were experimenting with beer (because we had been kids once ourselves). It took all the fun and mystique out of it, and neither Chris nor Camille was able to finish the glass served to them that day.

One of our Ambassadors in Brussels had been Leonard Firestone (yes of the tire family) who was generous to the Embassy staff in making his opera tickets available for our use. By the time we arrived in Portugal, Mark was crazy about opera, so we purchased our own box with seven seats. Would you believe we got the kids to attend operas in the jewel-like theatre in Lisbon? We did! They took their friends and sat in the back row where they would have some privacy from the audience. Chris always took his girlfriend. Her parents were so happy she was being exposed to opera. She turned into a musical comedy writer/producer, so they must have watched some of what was happening on stage.

Weather was almost always good. A marine climate meant some wind and rain, but it was usually warm during the day and cool in the evenings. Dinner parties were held outside within the walled garden. That was one of the most charming of our Foreign Service entertaining spaces.

I worked in the Embassy in part-time positions during three of the four years we were assigned there. Both of the positions I held were tailor-made for spouses. The first was editing *Tejo Talk*, the Embassy newsletter. Our family enjoyed driving around town 'discovering together.' I wrote about these mini trips and outlined possible excursions for others in the Embassy. One guy quipped, "I keep looking around for other Embassy people when I do your tours." I guess he didn't want to be caught dead or whatever.

The second job which I shared with another woman was working as the Community Liaison Office coordinator. We helped new employees get settled, adjusted and introduced to other families in the Embassy. We organized lectures on the history and culture of Portugal for both employees and family members. Most rewarding was working up walking tours of the City with our knowledgeable guide Hela Finberg leading the way. We were able to visit and experience neighborhoods most foreigners are not exposed to even in four years. We were the 'heart' of the administrative section of the Embassy.

Finally I was able to stop smoking the year before we left. It was not easy. The Embassy doctor agreed to give me sleeping pills for the first week so I wouldn't wander around town in the middle of the night looking for cigarettes. That helped considerably. Most older Portuguese men smoked, so I'd follow them around town (during the daytime) for the first few weeks breathing in their exhaled fumes.

What made me quit? A nurse told me she couldn't promise me lung cancer or a heart attack, but she would promise me emphysema if I didn't quit. Her father had just died from having smoked all his life. Her admonition was heartfelt, and I took her advice. I had tried to quit a dozen times before. This time it worked. Christopher had taken to wearing a gas mask and sticking the hose out the window where the exhaust from other cars smelled better than my cigarette smoke in the car. That made me quit.

At one point, I almost whacked off my finger trying to get a slice of bread cut from a loaf to get into my mouth quickly. My job-sharing partner who was an active AA member told me the only way to quit was to do whatever I had to do—just don't smoke. So I ate. Took a lot of walks. And after a few weeks, apples and oranges—not to mention all the delectable Portuguese foods—began tasting delicious in 3-D and living color.

Here's the rest of the story about being big fish in little ponds. I accompanied Mark on a visit to the Azores. The kids' biology teacher and his wife came to live in our house for a week to 'oversee' our two teenagers who adored them both. Off we went to see new housing construction where an earthquake had occurred a few years earlier.

On the island of *Terceira* while walking around the development of sturdier houses built hopefully to withstand the next earthquake, an Asian woman, the wife of the engineer administering the project, walked up to me, stuck out her hand to shake mine, and said, "Hello! I remember you from Angola."

I thought. *Angola? That was twenty years ago!* She went on to say she remembered eating delicious roast beef and American apple pie in our home. Wow! And I didn't think my presence was very necessary. She had actually remembered the menu. I don't recall if it was number one, two, three or four.

I remembered her face but not her name. She, her engineer husband, Mark and I had dinner together that evening, and we talked about the good old days in Angola. Some weren't good as several of our mutual friends were killed as a result of the guerilla war which raged just outside Luanda.

Many years after that dinner in Angola which she remembered so well, we were sent to Brussels where everything is of superior quality, from the construction of the buildings to the chocolate served with after-dinner coffee. Food is a main preoccupation of the entire Belgian population. One evening, several Belgians whom I'd never met were coming for dinner. I was having a bad day in my effort to quit smoking. I was surprised when the doorbell rang, and a florist delivered lovely orchids—before the party began. It put me back into the right frame of mind.

The guests arrived, and when we sat down to eat, they proceeded to talk about all the delicious meals they had consumed recently at local restaurants. The three main topics of conversation in Brussels were the proverbial war of words, Flemish or French, wet weather and food. Toward the end of the meal, the nice man who had sent the orchids told me the tomatoes were among the best he had eaten in a long time. He asked where I had purchased them.

The tomatoes! I had slaved over a hot stove for hours that day, and he liked the fresh tomatoes! The guests hadn't been gone five minutes when I rushed out of the house in search of a store selling cigarettes. Luckily, I've never been driven to drink.

I numbered menus in Belgium too. I didn't need to cross reference the folks at this particular dinner party, however. I probably wouldn't be inviting them back, and if I did, I'd just slice them up some fresh tomatoes. I wonder if the courtly orchid-sending Belgian will remember those tomatoes for 20 years like my Asian friend recalled that roast beef and apple pie. I'll bet she knew something about preparing food and hot stoves.

I have not talked about the 'issues' which Mark dealt with in these countries we served in. He got paid to be a diplomat. I was just a fellow traveler enjoying all the benefits of foreign travel but few responsibilities. He worked hard every day—it had been a calling of his to join the Foreign Service. Some politicians in the United States deride diplomats and call them cookie pushers and worse, but they are serious, very bright people carrying out the foreign policy of our country, sometimes against great odds and considerable danger. These bureaucrats are among the best and the brightest our country has to offer. It was a good life to be amongst them and their families over 32 years. Mark didn't take a sick day in all those years. That's how much he loved his job.

Oh, Brother!

This is the story of the most serendipitous occurrence of our lives.

After our four years in Portugal, we were reassigned to the States in the late eighties and were living in our Vienna, Virginia house. One summer day in 1989 Mark placed a phone call to the Prince William Cannons baseball club, a Yankee farm team located near Washington, D.C. The voice on the other end of the phone asked, "Yeah?"

Now, sit down and hold onto your seats.

"The Orioles aren't in town this weekend. I wondered if the Prince William Cannons will be," inquired Mark, anxious to see some live baseball.

"No, they're on the road. But, I can send you a schedule if you'd like so you can catch the next home game."

"Great!"

"Hold on a minute. Hafta find a pencil. It's not my job to take phone calls."

Mark waited several minutes. Having returned from a four-year tour in Portugal where they play soccer, he was anxious to see some good live baseball.

"OK, pencil found. Your name?"

After Mark gave his name and spelled it so the young man would get it right, there was dead silence on the other end of the line.

Finally, the voice asked, "Do you have any relatives in New Jersey?"

157

Mark responded, "No," but then he remembered that he had a half-brother, born of his father's first marriage, whom he had never met, and changed his answer to "Maybe, yes."

"Is his name Richard?"

"Well, yes."

"Is he a professor of psychology at Rutgers?"

"Yes, that's what I understand."

The young man responded, "I'm going to marry his daughter in November."

Mark, stunned, got some phone numbers and then hung up the phone. First there was silence—then tears as he told me the story.

Before we really absorbed it all, we 'flew' down to Prince William County in the car the following Sunday to meet the bride-to-be. Delightful can't describe her. Laura was the only child of Richard and Linda Lore. Putting all their eggs in this basket obviously was going to pay huge dividends one day.

A week later, there stood Linda and Dick at our front door. They drove to Virginia from New Jersey for our first meeting and lunch. Although Dick had seen his father only once as an adult, they had barely stepped inside the house when I noticed his mannerisms were so like his father's.

After those first encounters, our families were involved in making up for lost time. We attended Laura and Curt's wedding and sat at Table Number One. We tried hard to catch up on years of not knowing one another. We adults traveled together to several Elderhostels. Linda and Dick visited us in Brasilia during our tour there, came to our son Chris' wedding and visited us in Newport. We traveled to their picturesque retirement town, New Bern, North Carolina. The three Lore brothers, Richard, David and Mark, and their families did reunions together in Pennsylvania and Kentucky. It is sad to think that we didn't cross paths years earlier. Our kids and their cousin Diane would have enjoyed their other cousin Laura; and we could have watched all the four Lores grow.

Karl Lore, the daddy, (aka Leonard Carlton) accumulated three wives and four children. He was a charming but immature man.

There is no need to go through the whole business here of his falling in and out of love. However, because of this phone call, and because Curt happened to walk by a ringing phone and answered it that day, we had almost 20 years together before Dick's untimely death from cancer. Because we were adults, we knew what we had missed. We appreciated one another and discovered many common interests. How lucky to have made this connection. Dick left us too soon, but we'll cherish the memories and time we spent with him. Thank you, Curt, for answering the phone that day.

Brasilia, Once More!

We had an enjoyable few years in Virginia before leaving for our last overseas tour. I enjoyed this time of our lives. Our kids were becoming adults. Chris finished college and moved to California to do a year's internship with Toyota. Camille graduated from high school, began college and then moved to Savannah, Georgia, probably because her favorite art teacher lived there. Mark had a great job in the Department of State. I was able to find interesting jobs. The last one, particularly, was very fulfilling. As a former smoker, I was able to help the non-profit Action on Smoking and Health (ASH) with its litigation against that horrible Lady Nicotine.

John Banzhaf, founder and director of ASH, is the man who more than anyone else is responsible for getting smoking removed from public places—airlines, workplaces, restaurants and bars. He needed an executive secretary, and I got the job. I was terribly unhappy having to leave this job after just a couple of years. Two wonderful new friends worked at ASH, and I didn't want to leave them for another overseas tour. However, at that time in my life, I wasn't able to call all the shots.

It is fitting that our Foreign Service life ended where it began—in Brazil. Our second tour in Brasilia 26 years later, turned out to be a great experience and very different from our earlier time. A whole generation had been born and bred. We had several tours under our belts, our kids had grown and Brasilia, like us, had matured.

We were as seasoned as we were going to become. Our assigned quarters were the plushest we had experienced in the Foreign Service. We lived in a grand rambling low-slung house with six bedrooms and as many bathrooms. The upstairs veranda could hold 50 for sit down dinners, which could be doubled by using the downstairs patio. Located on the other side of the man-made lake, the residence for the deputy chief of mission (DCM) was built to be used for entertaining and for housing out-of-town official visitors. Gone were the days of cocktails for two in the small combined living/dining room in the two-bedroom apartment in Building 113 on the other side of the lake.

The DCM house came with servants to meet almost every need—a cook, maid, gardener, butler, driver and at the onset, a couple of guards. Additional help was hired when needed. Silver, china, crystal and linens were provided. What's not to love about that? In addition to hosting for official functions and entertaining, I had time for coffee klatches, women's groups, painting lessons, book clubs, teaching weaving and raising money for charities. We fit in a good deal of travel as well.

At night, Brasilia's city skyline from a distance looked enchanting. Because weather was agreeable most of the year, most entertaining took place outdoors. By the early 90s, the Brazilian Congress had vacated Rio, and all foreign embassies had re-located to Brasilia. Most of the other diplomats spent most of their time entertaining one another at cocktail parties. The Americans were always invited because they were the biggest embassy and generally knew best what was going on.

We had been in the house less than a week when one evening the *cul-de-sac* began buzzing and filled up with official and non-official cars alike. Our guard inquired as to what was happening next door. It was all hush-hush, but soon we knew from the sounds of the helicopter overhead, somebody important was landing in the neighbor's back yard.

Mark, ever the inquisitive reporter, found himself a porthole to proceedings and took notes on what the President of Brazil was telling his supporters next door. He was very excited at getting all this intelligence while sitting in the comfort of his own home. There was political tension in the air. President Collar de Mello was under a threat of impeachment by the Brazilian Congress because of alleged corruption. As I recall, we were still recovering from jet lag, but it looked like an exciting time was unfolding. Well after midnight, the festivities finally finished, and the Prez and his pilot helicoptered the few blocks to his home, and the cars drove away. Four months later President Collar was indeed impeached. (He is now rehabilitated, serving in the Brazilian Senate).

As all this official excitement was taking place, youngish nuns (between 70 and 85) at a retirement home for elderly nuns (over 85, I guess) conducted painting classes not far from our home. The story goes that Peruvian nuns had learned the equivalent of rosemaling, a type of Scandinavian decorative painting, from Spanish nuns and had passed on the know-how to these Brazilian sisters. I rushed over to this tranquil enclave during our first week in the city and began lessons in reverse glass painting as well as Brazilian/Peruvian rosemaling.

Since Mom was an accomplished early American decorative arts painter who spent decades painting after she turned 60, I thought maybe this ability was part of my DNA, so I spent three years painting twice a week with the nuns and their entourage of foreign and Brazilian women. It helped improve my Portuguese, although the new vocabulary wasn't particularly useful at cocktail parties unless another painter happened to be in the crowd. I met a whole different segment of the population and enjoyed my time with them immensely.

Another activity, begun as an offshoot of the American Women's Club, was the Friday afternoon sewing group (lovingly referred to as the stitch and bitch club). This cast of characters evolved into a sisterhood of the first order. Often women of other nationalities were involved in the group, and sometimes membership exceeded 25 on a Friday afternoon. The core group during the three years we lived in Brasilia became very tight friends. Without our realizing what was happening, our meetings, which lasted about three hours on Friday afternoons, grew into a support group. In addition extraordinary quilters perfected their craft.

Many of us have continued to stay in touch with one another over the years. Those of us in the Washington, DC area try to meet once in awhile. Seeing one another has proven to be more difficult than it was when we were all in Brasilia together. What a luxury it was to pass Friday afternoons kibitzing with friends, embroidering, mending or stitching quilts. Of course, we had the odd painter who thought that craft was close enough to sewing to participate. These women became family to one another as we shared time together in the hinterland of Brazil.

The American Women's Club book group met at our residence each month. It worked well, because we could meet on the covered veranda all year long. You know how cicadas invade the United States every 17 years? They show up every year in Brazil. The Swiss Ambassador's wife had just arrived in Brasilia and attended her first book club meeting at the height of the cicadas mating and courtship calls. Ten minutes into our book discussion, she demanded I get those bugs to stop making so much noise. I certainly would have honored her request had I possessed such powers. However, they kept up their scissor-grinding sounds and almost drove us all crazy that day.

We learned after that three-year posting that Chris and Camille—now young adults—were not at all pleased we had gone off to Brazil without them. I think we forgot to tell them after they grew up, they wouldn't be traveling around with us any longer. But, they coped. They both visited us at post which was special indeed. By this time, we could afford to buy plane tickets so we could leave our overseas posting when stateside matters needed attention. That meant I returned to the States each year to visit family which was very different from our early years in the service when we could only afford to return home every two years (depending on the needs of the service).

Dad died four months before we left for our last tour. Mom lived in a retirement community and telephoned every Sunday afternoon. No longer did I feel so far from home, and she didn't feel so far away from us. We didn't have phone service to the United States when we lived in Brazil in the 1960s except in case of emergency when one could use an Embassy phone to place and patch a call to the States.

During this second tour, we were able to travel around the country more because of Mark's position. State Department officials told young officers when they first joined the Foreign Service that each should drive from coast to coast in the USA to get a feel for its size and diversity. They would have a better idea of the enormity of the United States and the diversity of the people they would be representing. The same could have been said of Brazil. It is as varied as our own country. We were able to visit most regions of Brazil, meet the friendliest people on the planet, taste the cuisine, admire the landscapes, hear the music, watch the dance, enjoy the ethnicity of the country, and, yes, to see some of the Amazon, Brazil's greatest hit.

Although we have good friends from that first tour in Rio when we were all novices-in-training together, some of my best Foreign Service friends came from that second Brasilia tour. We were grown-ups now and spent little time worrying about the small stuff.

During our first week in Brasilia, I met an American jeweler who had married a Brazilian woman sometime between our two assignments there. He, his wife and daughters did a land office business selling semi-precious stones and jewelry. He must have gotten bored at some point, because as a sideline, he built weaving looms—beautiful four-harness looms of indigenous Brazilian wood.

By the time we arrived in 1992 he had constructed at least a dozen looms, but no one in town knew how to weave. When he discovered I was a weaver, he asked if I could teach some people to weave so he could sell them his looms. So, we set up a half dozen looms in one of the rooms of our residence, and I taught beginning weaving to women in the American Women's Club (a misnomer because at least half the women were of other nationalities). He then sold all the looms at very modest prices. They were shipped all over the world when these new weavers returned to their home countries. Problem solved. Looms now had weavers. I continue to be grateful for weaving in my life, begun in Brussels during our bicentennial year.

Some Still Married
After All These Years...

Mark and I celebrated our 30th wedding anniversary in 1994. It was such a thrill to have my matron of honor cousin Rita and her husband, Don, spend a couple of weeks with us during this time. We managed to get away to an old colonial city near Rio for a weekend—even though the pre-pre-pre advance team for Vice President Gore's impending visit was in Brasilia assessing the situation. Somebody from Washington asked Mark to return to Brasilia, but his wedding anniversary celebration won out. He told them the Embassy was covered, and he was otherwise occupied. God bless him!

Between Ambassadors, Mark served as the *Charge' d'affaires,* or acting ambassador. During this time, Vice President Gore, his wife and entourage made a weekend visit to Latin America. We took care of them when they arrived from Argentina passing through Brasilia on their return trip to the States. Mark had dealt with Presidents and administration officials all during his Foreign Service career, but it was the first time I had the opportunity to escort wives whose husbands held important positions in our government. During that tour, in addition to Mrs. Gore, I also spent time with the wives of Colin Powell, Secretary of Defense Perry and General McCaffrey—lovely, intelligent women all.

I got a six-hour taste of what our Presidents, Vice Presidents, cabinet officers and other high-ranking government officials tolerate on a daily basis. When I accompanied Tipper Gore during their hours in Brasilia, I learned how one's favorite treats are waiting for one in the official car, how nobody gets in and out of the limos until the Secret Service tells them they can, proper seating protocol, and on it goes. Tipper was delightful. She seemed somewhat frustrated because her cell phone couldn't reach their kids in the States. I reminded her we were in the middle of Brazil—maybe the satellites weren't positioned correctly. Of course, that was almost 20 years ago, and improved technology has roared ahead since then.

After the official State dinner at the Foreign Office with Brazil's Foreign Minister, we attended a Town Meeting where Vice-President Gore answered questions about America's foreign policy for a representative group of Brazilians. He introduced his wife as 'Tipper Gore.' She whispered to me that after all these years, he could leave off the last name, but he always said, 'Tipper Gore.' Funny about husbands, isn't it?

Returning with them to the airport for their flight back to the States, Mark and I sat in jumper seats in the limo facing Tipper and the Vice President. They had to be exhausted, but do you know what they did? They necked! I was blown away by this, heartened by it and frustrated because I didn't know which way to turn to avert my eyes. I think that says so much about our officials. They are real people. They knew they were on the last leg of their trip, and they finally relaxed with one another. It turns out they will be getting a divorce after 40 years of marriage. That makes them into real people indeed.

Life in the Fast Lane...
Newport, Here We Come!

Life after the Foreign Service began before our Foreign Service life had finished. Rather than trying for a possible small-country-in-Africa ambassadorial assignment, we decided that an academic stateside posting would be a more enjoyable transition to fast-approaching retirement.

Living in the states, we would see another part of the country as we did with the 10-month tour in Wisconsin. Of all the wonderful places to be assigned, we landed in Newport, Rhode Island. Mark taught strategy/policy seminars at the Naval War College for two years. Early in our time in Newport, Chris married Barbara Tidey, a lovely woman with whom he worked at the Toyota Central Atlantic Region headquarters.

We thoroughly enjoyed everything about Newport except winter. Friends and family visited us over the time we spent there in a tremendous half house with five bedrooms. Two blocks from all Newport action, the house was divided with the landlord and landlady next door who kept us apprised on all things cultural in this New England setting, the former playground for the extraordinarily rich. Tourism was the number one business in Newport, and we spent two years appreciating it all. Were it not for its cold, snowy, dark winters and the occasional nor'easter we might have hung around forever.

Several Foreign Service people have happily settled there.

Finally, I was back weaving with two different guilds. I found that in the coldest parts of our country, people continue to enjoy crafts perhaps because of their long winters. It's the same with the Scandinavians who are among the world's best weavers. I was weaving with others once again. What fun.

Before we left for Brasilia in 1992, we had bought a 1790s restored house in the city of Winchester—75 miles west of where we were living in Vienna. The Shenandoah Valley was destined to become our retirement home. I had always wanted to live in a log house, so my dream was practically fulfilled as this house retained an exposed log wall after restoration. The Peter Miller house was both historic and cozy—that oft used description for small. Winchester itself offered everything we would need in retirement with a university with music conservatory at one end of town and a medical center at the other. An organization existed for every kind of cause or pursuit. A thriving Unitarian Universalist Church was located just down the road, the liberal beacon in the Valley.

Winchester did become our retirement home, but the old house wasn't conducive to our needs at this time of our lives. We did move in for a few months, but there was no place to put the loom except in the middle of the living room floor. It just wasn't going to work. We had acquired too much stuff and were mindful of the need for psychological as well as physical space for each of us. We sold the 'charmer' to a friend after a number of years of renting it to people who loved aged houses. About a half mile up the road, we found another dwelling which was 150 years newer. We've been here almost 11 years now, so it is time for a garage sale. We have too much stuff because we haven't been able to clear things out with moves once in awhile.

Mark and I have joined many organizations here and have made new, remarkable friends. It was the right retirement choice. Three splendid things happened for me—well, more than that, but you don't want to hear about all of them. I wove dozens of rag rugs; I took up the fiddle again after decades of ignoring it; and I got involved in both writing groups and local social justice organizations. Mark became ensconced in Magic Lantern Theater movies, a local movie society; he investigated Winchester's history through various historical organizations; and he taught international relations as an adjunct professor at the university. What catholic interests he has. What curiosity. And, he says I wear him out.

I didn't expect this to be the best time of my life, but it is. I wonder why retirees keep this a secret.

The Re-run Spice Set

Carol and Bill, old friends from our days in Brussels, visited a while back.

On their way out the door, Bill noticed the spice rack hanging on the wall. I think he had seen it many times in the past 30 years, but he asked about its history. He recognized the item probably came from Belgium. His admonition was, "Write about it and tape the spice rack's story to the back of it so the kids don't toss it out one day."

This item was probably 100 years old when we met up with it in the mid 1970s. Produced in Czechoslovakia around the turn of the 20th century, it was designed for French-speaking countries with the spice jars labeled in French. Six large jars hold staples like coffee, rice, flour, sugar, and the smaller ones are marked for spices. Additionally, bottles on either side hold oil and vinegar complete with stoppers. How European!

Here's the story. Our Brussels commune had begun a series of flea markets on the first Saturday morning of each month. The site was in front of the ancient municipal buildings, a picturesque and perfect location. I'll bet someone on the commune council found himself burdened with a basement or an attic full of stuff he'd like to unload. Only Americans were so crass as to hold garage sales in Belgium. The face-saving method for unloading unwanted stuff for Europeans must have been through flea markets. In any case, we missed the first one held the previous month, which probably contained untold numbers of incredibly wonderful old, valuable European treasures.

The second market, which we attended that Saturday morning wasn't too shabby either. Mom and Dad were visiting at the time, so it was a tourist destination, of course. Dad's sister, my Auntie Bum, had asked him to watch for Delft tiles during his visit. What caught his eye were the blue and white tiles on top of a grungy, broken down cardboard box at the back of the vendor's space.

"Sandy, please ask him about the tiles." Dad wasn't too confident of using his high school and college French this many years after the learning. (He admitted he could ask the question but wouldn't understand the answer).

A discussion took place between the vendor and me. He climbed over other *objects d'art* to reach the box of tiles. These tiles were lodged in a pine rack with two shelves and four hooks. The shelves held all the jars. Although we didn't unwrap it all, the vendor assured me it was 'complete'. I asked him how much it cost, and when he told me, I enthusiastically agreed to the purchase without hesitation.

He kept assuring us of its completeness. I really didn't care how complete it was. It was filthy dirty which concerned me more. He must have crawled up into his great-grandmother's attic to encounter boxes of no longer used stuff, which may have been sitting there for decades.

We headed straight home with our find. Mom was anxious to get started on restoring the wood, which was unbelievably grimey. Dad figured he'd still find Auntie Bum some tiles without all this extra stuff like jars and racks.

We spent the rest of the day scrubbing the jars and sanding the wood. You would have thought we had found a King's crown as we cleaned away looking for the pine's golden luster.

Our hard work finished, we discovered one of the small jars was missing its lid. Hmmm, it wasn't complete after all. It didn't make much difference to me—the lidless jar could hold paper clips or rubber bands or be useful in one way or another. I promptly forgot about the jar lid. When the next month's market rolled around, Mom and Dad were home in Illinois, but I walked the few blocks to check

171

out the classy community bazaar anyway.

The vendor was no longer in his location. Another person was there—a young French-speaking girl who asked, "Are you the American who bought a spice set here last month?" I acknowledged I was. She said last month's vendor had mistakenly left a spice lid in another box. The person who bought that other box of goods realized it didn't belong to anything she had purchased, so she brought it back to the vendor. This morning, the vendor stopped by with the lid and asked me to give it to the American who had purchased what she thought was a complete spice set.

Here is the rest of the story: My brother Doug and his wife Judy with their kids Trish and David visited us in Madison soon after we were settled. Doug had never seen anything like the spice set and fell in love with it. He proceeded to collect spice sets from that day forward. He had some very elegant ones in his possession when he died. Ours isn't elegant—just complete. It has moved with us wherever we have lived. I would have willed it to Doug had he outlived me.

Where Were You?

September 11, 2001, we emerged from the little camper out in the yard after a good night's sleep. On the way into Mike and Karen's home near Plano, Illinois, the smell of perking coffee permeated the air. Mark and I commented to one another on the perfectly cloudless azure sky above and the beautiful day ahead.

Before we had consumed coffee, the calm country quiet was disrupted by a 15-year-old Rachael looking dazed and perplexed as she tripped down the steps from her home-school perch upstairs choking out, "A plane has slammed into the Twin Towers in New York." Being the consummate New Yorker, Mark quickly educated us on a 'similar' incident in the mid-forties when a small military plane flew into the Empire State Building. 'Pilot error' went through our collective minds. If there's nobody to blame, there's always the pilot, right?

Incredulous all, everyone hurried upstairs to watch the unfolding news. Although numb, we had a commitment to drive Mom 25 miles east to Naperville for a dental appointment. En route we learned via NPR that the other tower was hit by a plane and the Pentagon was burning.

A fourth plane had gone down in Pennsylvania before Mom had finished at the dentist,. The President announced from an unknown location that terrorism had struck our shores. We knew our lives were changing faster than we could process the knowledge.

Yet the sky was still gloriously blue with no airplanes or jet streams to be seen. The horror of it all shook our corner of the planet like a tsunami. Our terror continues to arrive via the television screen by way of Iraq, Pakistan, Afghanistan, Madrid or London. How can we still get a good night's sleep?

The Menagerie Over the Years

Dad brought the surprise puppy home to Mom several years before my birth, so in a sense, Steffie—her name was shortened for everyday use—was their first kid and I, the second. I am told Steffie acquired her Russian names over a period of time. Steffie's whole name was Steffie Annovich Constantine Senkunyunski Nicolai Sokolof Obalochko Senko Brian. Excuse the spellings.

Perhaps they were Russian names because Dad was completely enraptured by Tschaikovsky or perhaps it was because he had a card-carrying communist friend who exerted some influence. We'll never know.

In any case Steffie was a fluffy toy spitz, a small dog to have such a long name. She was all white except for one ear lightly touched with brown. She had quite a repertoire of tricks. Of course she did the usual things like fetching, rolling over and playing dead. The most amazing thing to me as a child, however, was that with every passing year, she knew her age. Mom or Dad would just ask her, "Steffie, how old are you?" She'd tilt her head as if to make sure she understood the question. Then, she would start barking one...two...three...four... five and so on. She always stopped at the right number of barks.

I believe I was grown and married by the time I knew the magic of this trick. When she arrived at the correct number, my parents would reach out their hands to pet her, smile and say, "That's a good girl, Steffie."

When I was born, Steffie was already five years old. Doug and I played 'dress-up' with Steffie. How can a dog tolerate playing with little kids like that? I have a picture of her with a scarf—or rather babushka—tied around her head.

Steffie's story ends in 1946 in Joliet. I don't remember her being sick, but I do remember her slowing down and becoming very inactive. Maybe she died of old age. She left a huge void in our family when she died.

Here's Dad's obituary to his dog published in the Chicago Daily News:

Steffie died last night and with her death came the end of an era in our family. Steffie was our little toy Spitz with one brown ear, a sunny disposition and a heart as big as that full round moon I see outside my window as I write this. Had she lived until Thanksgiving, she would have been 12, a good long life, anyway for a dog, I keep telling myself. But nostalgia grips me, and I think back over those 12 years, realizing that I, too, am getting old.

When we got her, she fit nicely in my overcoat pocket. And the first night she cried so from her box in the kitchen that we finally decided to let her be one of the family and keep warm at the foot of our bed. There she slept for almost five years, until our firstborn arrived. "Get rid of the dog," our friends told us, "she'll be jealous of the baby." But she wasn't...instead, she welcomed the little girl and was glad with us over her arrival. Three years later, she helped us prepare for the coming of a son, and since has been the constant companion and watchful playmate of both.

So, tonight, is it any wonder that the 7-year-old called down to her mother and me, "I can't go to sleep, because Steffie's dead?" And I, too, feel that somehow in the cosmic scheme of things, there's a new star in the heavens tonight, watching over the new grave back of the house, piled high with glacial rocks, marking the spot where Steffie sleeps.

W.E. Brian

I've had a dozen pets since Steffie, but it was she who played a big part in my young life. She was one of the best friends my little brother and I ever had. Even now when I look up at the night sky, I wonder which star might be the one shining down where Steffie sleeps.

Our kids liked having pets too. Chris as a little boy told the nursery school teacher he'd surely like to have a pet cat. The guinea pig just didn't cut it. Sugar joined the family within days. She was a fixed, nondescript, black, domestic shorthaired cat. You see them around once in awhile. It turned out Chris was and still is highly allergic to cats. Sugar the Cat traveled to Morocco with us. Sugar had a dog brother in Morocco named Brownie. Yes, the kids named the pets.

Sugar was a good cat and didn't make waves of any kind except to make Chris sneeze on contact. All I remember about Brownie was his color, his rambunctious manner and his insatiable appetite. When the cook left the oven door ajar, Brownie was able to open it completely, yank out the chicken, roast or leg of lamb and gulp down the whole thing while everybody else in the household was otherwise occupied. What a dog. He stayed with the house when we left Morocco, because the new family wanted to keep him. Brownie and Sugar both lived out their lives in north Africa.

Over the years, we extended hospitality and hearth to several dogs. Sometimes they bit little kids. That wouldn't do, because we had at least two kids in the house all the time. One lovely dog arrived from the pound pregnant, so she didn't hang around long. We didn't need many dogs, just one.

During our tour in Belgium, we acquired that rather fancy Cairn terrier in Nottingham, England. Unfortunately for Geordie McVitie, his ancestors had been inbred, which resulted in his having bad manners and acting slightly crazy. He barked incessantly. That's not a good thing if you live in a townhouse with German neighbors who wish to sleep at night. As a family, we were already high strung and didn't need extra help from a pet.

On returning to the states from our four years in Belgium, we stayed in a motel outside Washington, D.C. for a few nights until we left to spend the summer in Illinois. Dogs and motel rooms aren't meant for one another. Geordie rocketed out the door one morning and onto Route 50. Mark and the kids chased him up the highway. I stayed in the motel and watched with horror. They caught the dog. Luckily, highway construction was taking place, and Geordie fell into a sand pit. We think he also had gone a bit round the bend staying in a small cage in Heathrow Airport for a couple of weeks.

There's a Geordie story wherever we lived. This was the summer the kids and I spent six weeks with Mom and Dad in Naperville. Of course, Geordie went with us. Mark stayed in Washington to do preparatory work for graduate economics. Mom and Dad lived within two blocks of Ogden Avenue, a very busy street with two lane traffic in both directions. Yes, somehow or another, Geordie got loose and headed for the road. The four kids, Chris and Camille and their two Brian cousins, Tricia and David, took off after him. Camille held her hand up to stop traffic going east on the busy commuter road to Chicago. The kids careened between cars and caught Geordie. None of the adults at the time of this incident knew what was going on. Luckily, all the kids and the dog survived. Geordie didn't roam again—at least in Illinois.

He moved to Madison, Wisconsin with us for that 10-month academic year. Mark took him to YMCA dog-training classes where he did very well until the final test. He didn't do a thing right that night. He actually pooped instead of following instructions. Mark came home so deflated muttering, "Dumb dog, dumb dog."

When we moved back to Virginia, Geordie survived the two years we lived in Fairfax but didn't survive living outside Clifton. Evidently, being high strung, he was frightened by the vacuum sweeper one day and tore out the door again, this time onto a dirt road only to be hit by a neighbor's truck. He was buried beneath the trees of our home. We were all inconsolable. It was so quiet without Geordie's yipping.

My response was to issue an ultimatum to the kids, "There will be no more dogs for awhile." Only two weeks before Geordie's demise, Chris and Camille's rabbits had dropped dead in their hutches. Unfortunately, they had painted the hutches with lead-based paint

178

which the rabbits ate. The kids had now gone through too much trauma losing all their pets in such a short period of time. Therefore, we would be a family of four without a pet for a while.

That dictum lasted 24 hours. A neighbor's prize young English bulldog had been impregnated by a 15-year-old Labrador retriever who had hobbled across a fence to do the deed. The vet suggested to them that birthing would give her needed experience for the time when she would produce future prizewinners. Eleven pups later, she probably had the necessary experience. The family needed to find homes for all these unexpected puppies, so we helped them out. Chris chose and named Corky, a strawberry blond male, who matched his hair color. Yes, Camille chose and named Chauncey, a coal black girl puppy whose coat matched her hair. Each was thrilled with his own puppy.

My brother Mike and his future wife Karen visited us in Clifton during this time, and Karen helped Chris and Camille figure out how much wood would be required to build a little fence so the pups could be outdoors but not close to the road. They might live to old age that way. The kids did the math and built the enclosure themselves. What kids! The last time I looked, the sturdy edifice was still there behind the garage, almost hidden from the road.

Soon we were on the move again. Corky and Chauncey arrived in Portugal several weeks before we did. Until our arrival, they stayed in an upscale kennel near the beach with an ocean view. We arrived on a Sunday, and we'd no sooner left the airport than we began driving around the little seaside village where the kennel was located to listen for their barks. We didn't have an address for their vacation location, but we knew we'd recognize their barks if we heard them. We were unsuccessful and needed to wait to retrieve them from their palatial digs the next day.

Their life in Portugal was as diverse in housing as ours. The first place was a party house, and they could roam freely in the back yard, because it wasn't meant to be used, just looked at from on high. A walled fence about ten feet high enclosed the garden at the next house, so they were safe romping around the garden there. It was a beautiful, lush garden with rosemary bushes and flowering plants ringing the space. The last time I walked them together in Lisbon, they dragged me across an intersection while chasing a cat. I was flat on my tummy, and because they never looked back and were oblivious to my situation, they didn't stop when I yelled at them. That was our last stroll together. At least no cars or motorcycles were tearing through the intersection at that moment, and I'm here to talk about the experience. They chased both cats and squirrels. Sometimes they caught them. Imagine what happened next. I'll not tell you.

They seemed to have as many lives as cats. Corky got caught whirling around a current in the ocean one Sunday morning, but Mark was able to rescue him.

They lived to be 15-years-old. They accompanied us to Brasilia where they also lived a luxurious life years later. Chris learned from a vet when Corky died that he had been shot, and the bullet had missed his heart but not by much. Some people thought they were ugly dogs, but they weren't. They were beautiful both inside and out with a charming easygoing demeanor common to labs. They could scare people with their bulldog faces, but we considered that a real plus.

The dogs returned to the states after their Brazilian sojourn. Chris and Barb took Corky into their home after marriage, and Chauncey accompanied us to Newport as Camille wasn't in a position to take care of her at that time. It seemed so strange to us that when they were with each other in their later years, (Thanksgiving and Christmas in Newport), they didn't know they had been littermates and vied for territory in our big old Newport half house. There was space for everybody, but I guess they couldn't understand that. After all, they were just dogs—perfect half-breed dogs!

Some people have said that life begins when the kids leave home and the dog dies. Maybe so. After many years of 'freedom' without a pet, we took in a fine old cat, already trained and mature.

Mango is an aging, fifteen pound, furry, orange, mature cat with white socks and a white bib. He is circumspect, cautious, careful and demure if I may be allowed to use that word for a male cat.

FROM OREOS TO OLIOS

We don't know the real beginnings of Mango's life except that Robyn (his last 'mother') said he was found scraggly, in need of veterinary care for a leg abscess, and wandering somewhere in New York State. He evidently found Cindy's home where cats lived and kept himself alive on their food. She took him in although she already had many cats. She knew she couldn't take on another for many reasons—space, vet bills, food, and everything else one must consider with a pet. She called her Virginia friend and fellow animal lover Robyn and asked her to take in this orange and white cat that she had named 'Pumpkin.'

Robyn loves all animals. I doubt that she has ever turned any away. I'm grateful she didn't say no to this particular cat. She met Cindy halfway between New York and Winchester where 'Pumpkin' changed hands and names.

Robyn returned to her Winchester menagerie with this cat. She later told me some of the names she had considered for him—keeping it Pumpkin (too common), Paprika (too many syllables) and then finally she hit on Mango (perfect). He and three other cats lived with Robyn for five years. Because of 'feline disagreements,' the cats were given individual rooms in Robyn's house; Mango, evidently the alpha male, had the basement all to himself. Then, circumstances beyond Mango's control arose. Robyn fell in love with Ron, got married and moved to Florida. She had too many pets to take along, so Mango became our cat. How fortunate we were.

He arrived just before Easter three years ago. Robyn and the cat broker Alice brought him from the vet's where he had been for a spa treatment. Decked out in his pastel striped spring scarf-like bib for his arrival at his new home, he looked leery of what was going down. Although shy, he sat on my lap where he stayed quite happily. Robyn provided all the necessary *accoutrements*—cat specific bowls, a bed (his favorite old chair), medicines, a cat box for travel, his wire brush, and his favorite tuna tasting treats. It was evident she had loved him and cared for him well. Robyn guessed Mango was about ten then.

All our retirement routines changed with Mango's arrival. We became staff and lost the status of masters of our own fate. Mango was mature when he joined the family and has not been instructed on anything. Can one teach old cats new tricks? No, but this old cat is teaching us.

From OREOS *to* OLIOS

PART III

March of the OLIOS!

Since weaving has played such an important part in my life for years, I must tell you about it now before I go on to our life after retirement.

Beginning in Belgium, weaving was the thread woven through the rest of our time in the Foreign Service. Mom and Dad were visiting, and together we made the trek to Holland where small floor looms were manufactured just over the border. I purchased a little four-harness loom of rather dubious design. In 1979 after taking courses related to weaving at the University of Wisconsin, I bought an eight-harness Gilmore loom. It was a jewel, or as my professor and friend Joyce Marques Carey alleged, the 'Cadillac of looms.'

These days, I have one of Dad's smaller looms which I've used for rug weaving during the past 18 years. He had asked me which of his looms I'd like to have when he and Mom downsized, and I chose the 'small' loom, a Union Loom No. 36, rather than one of his large Newcomb looms with flying shuttles.

This loom, which I use for all projects these days, is simple in design and construction and is as strong as an ox—or maybe a battleship. In any case it is very sturdy and can take a considerable amount of hard beating which is needed for rug weaving. I've spent many hours throwing shuttles and beating fabric into rugs on this loom. This is my kind of meditation.

I belonged to various guilds at various times from 1976 on. Both

185

Potomac Craftsmen and Waterford Weavers were wonderful teaching guilds, and I was able to benefit from them when we lived in northern Virginia. When we spent two years in Rhode Island, I joined two guilds which were full of outstanding weavers. I was hooked on rug weaving from those folks who take this stuff very seriously indeed. Here in the Valley, there's a dynamic bunch of weavers in a guild called Blue Ridge Spinners and Weavers. They are a young, creative and enthusiastic bunch of women. I became a charter member of their guild, and they wore me out!

After retiring to Winchester, I wove rugs with a passion. These were rag rugs but made with new fabric so color and design could become an integral part of this utilitarian household item. For the first few years here in Winchester, I wove non-stop and produced dozens of rugs which I sold at various craft fairs and the Winchester City Market.

Then, I rediscovered my violin, and I learned one cannot weave and fiddle at the same time. So, the loom is waiting for me to pick up a shuttle again, but the violin continues to call me daily. If I ever lose interest in fiddling, or if I become less compulsive about it, I'll head back to that dressed loom waiting in its special room. I'll never be bored. I may wear out, but I don't think I'll rust out!

Finally, No More Upchucking

I used to vomit before performing with my violin. I put it away for many years, because I didn't like to vomit. Then, I brought out the fiddle after decades of storage. Let me tell you what happened. With help from my friends and two patient, kind women, Pat O'Boyle and Murphy Henry, I got started playing all over again. Now I would choose which kind of music to play.

Traditional dance music from the British Isles was my first new love. Scandinavian dance music isn't far behind. And, bluegrass holds a special place in my heart because the musicians who play it are some of my favorite people. My fellow UU friend Deirdre got me involved in several groups playing music and urged me to count. One must count if one plays music with others. Life is good—very good. We two are now working assiduously on becoming Scandinavian dance musicians.

One particular Sunday morning, I was playing without accompaniment at the end of a church service of poetry. Before I left home, this is what happened while sitting at our dining room table.

The curtains wafted back and forth, back and forth to the rhythmic hum of both fans blowing hot air making it cooler for the curtains and me. With noisy birds chirping happily, my attention was diverted from staying cool to the scene outside the window. Look at all that green—the leaves on the trees, the ivy growing up the tree trunks and the uninvited poison ivy with its tentacles reaching out to set up multi-level residences all over our hillside waiting in anticipation of attacking humans at the slightest provocation. That distracted me momentarily. I stopped to scratch the imaginary itch.

The fresh sweet cantaloupe and healthy '1000-grain' toast with real butter and cinnamon taste so good. I try to relax about playing the fiddle at church. Nerves were working overtime. Other body parts are aging, why not nerves also? Agitation over playing in public has existed since I was a kid. Because I play about the same in public as in private, this shouldn't be a problem. There will be no lasting ill effects on anyone hearing my music this morning. The sounds waft upward toward the heavens.

Past public performances drifted through my mind. One Easter Sunday sunrise service, I wore my new red dress with matching jacket embellished with pearls and other sparklers. Big mistake! With jubilant organ accompaniment, I played 'Christ the Lord has risen Today,' with unanticipated and undisciplined percussion coming from the jacket whenever the violin moved a fraction. It was noisy—even extending to the front rows of the church. At 8th grade graduation, I played a solo to my class with my back to the audience hoping they wouldn't see or hear me. A fellow classmate remembers both incidents. Every five years or so, he sees fit to remind me of my past fiddling.

Then, I wondered, *does a fiddle, the instrument of the devil, belong in church?* I believe that if I called the instrument a violin, it would be all right to play in church. Both violins and churches are sacred. 'Fiddles' might not make the sacred cut.

The prism in the window caught my eye. Hanging in an east window to catch the morning rays, it sparkles without prompting—even on days when no sun pours in. Today, on the right, there was a bright white 'star' twinkling behind it. I kept watching. It appeared then disappeared and appeared again. I peeked again out of the corner of my eye.

I thought, *now there.* That must be Mom twinkling down at me telling me to "Go play that fiddle. Do the best you can. Make it sing." She had the most affirming nature of anybody I've ever known.

And then, oh, my goodness, here comes another twinkling 'star'

188

behind the prism. That has to be Dad! I wonder what message he is sending. I'll bet he's telling me not to play flat. He thought I played flat most of the time. I still do sometimes. He'd be tickled that I was playing my fiddle in the Unitarian Universalist Church. He once told me not to pay any attention to those Universalists as they were nuts. Now I am one. Maybe he was right. Here I am receiving messages from a prism.

Yes, here it comes—a third twinkling 'star'—probably from Mr. Herath, my former violin teacher. He, who launched my playing 60 years ago, would be pleased to know that I had picked up the fiddle once more. He repeated over many years, "Every note should sound like a pearl." I didn't get it. He kept repeating it. Maybe from his twinkling star he is shooting me pearls from the heavens.

I am thrilled to be fiddling again. These bright sparkling prism lights are giving me exactly the boost I need for playing this morning. Only two people will know the 18th century Scottish tune—Deirdre with whom I play music and Mark who has endured the practicing of said piece. I know the notes—I could play them without written music, but I have enough to worry about without subjecting myself or anybody else to that.

So, I'm ready. With those three bright stars glimmering down on me from the lovely, multifaceted, multicolored prism, how can I fail? I've regained some courage. I'm ready to go. There will be no vomiting.

With breakfast over, it's time to head out the door. First, I grab some Chap Stick. That is another sign of nervousness—dry lips. A new flavor? Something is very wrong. The Chap Stick has a new distinct taste. Whoops! I've just covered my lips with glue from a glue stick. Will the prism glow see me through or not?

In the end I played, well enough, and my dear friend Naomi told me after the service that was one more tune I've played that she doesn't recognize. I told her the congregation would be in real trouble if I played something they thought they had heard before.

So, there you are. My new passion is launched and running smoothly. I am having way too much fun in retirement!

189

Nature and Me

It turns out I prefer looking out the window at nature rather than messing around in it. I like watching our healthy weeds grow when nothing else does. I like hearing rain drops hitting the windows in rapid succession. It's soothing and safe—indoors looking out.

The other day, nature and I bumped a thousand heads on the eastern edge of the Blue Ridge Mountains. I ventured outdoors—to the Sky Meadows State Park near Delaplane in Fauquier County—to fiddle away the afternoon and bring some Celtic Heir sounds to the park's Sunday afternoon visitors. Under a big old tree, firmly rooted in the back yard of the 1860 historic house, we made music. Our tunes were accompanied by resident song birds. The audience was appreciative. The scene couldn't have been more charming under the tree or more bucolic looking off in any direction.

If there was rain in the threatening sky, it passed us by. To make up for the lack of rain, the gnats were out in full force. That small parcel of old land undoubtedly has more gnats per square inch than any other place in the whole Commonwealth of Virginia. And, they were very, very hungry.

They didn't care a thing about the music. They swarmed all around my head, into my nose, ears and eyes. And all the time I jigged and reeled away. Once, I felt I might be almost blinded, but then I realized that gnat was at my bad eye, which wouldn't affect seeing the music in any way, so I kept on fiddling.

I don't like gnats. Never have. If there is an earthly reason for gnats to 'grow and multiply,' I can't figure out what it is. If there is a god, why did he plan gnats? He had more important work to do than arranging for a population of flying bugs who take up too much of my space when I'm in the great outdoors, under a tree and fiddling. OK, personal god, answer me that one!

I read that "Male gnats often assemble together in large mating swarms, particularly at dusk, called a 'ghost'." That comes straight from Wikipedia. Those low slung clouds probably tricked those male gnats into thinking it was biting time. In any case the music wafted straight from the instruments to God's ears—with or without interference from gnats.

I did recover after a great supper of pizza and a nice warm shower and yet another shampoo—the second one that day. Now, I ask you, if you were a gnat, which some god put here, on a July summer's day, wouldn't you rather be napping?

When I'm queen, I'll pass a law that says "gnats will nap on Sunday afternoons—even the males." There will be no exceptions—especially while songbirds sing to a fiddle and a harp making music outdoors under a big old tree.

A Dedicated Tune

Recently our little trio called Chicks with Attitude accepted an invitation to play music for The Willows at Meadow Branch, an assisted living facility here in town. We prepared the usual number of tunes—music for thirty to forty minutes. When we arrived, we learned it was a church service, and we would have time only for three songs.

The gathering place at The Willows was crowded by their standards. Several folks were wheeled in. As always, most of the residents were women. I believe four elderly men wore 'Dad' pins in honor of Father's Day. The gathering was called 'Summerfest' to honor fathers.

One early arrival left before he got in the door. "I notice three crosses there. Is this a church service?" he gruffly asked.

Perky Molly, the activities director, explained, "It's a special service for Father's Day."

"It looks like a church service. Is it?"

"Yes, but everyone is welcome. Please come on in."

"No, I don't attend church services here or anyplace else."

I thought—*poor guy. Here he is stuck in an assisted living situation. Maybe he's Jewish. Maybe he's an atheist or a Unitarian Universalist like me. In any case, here he is—stuck.* I knew how he felt. I didn't feel all that comfortable. 'Summerfest' didn't seem to fit the occasion somehow.

I hadn't expected Sarah and Abraham to be there too. The chaplain made them the centerpiece of his sermon entitled 'Not Older but Better'. Remember, he was talking to a group of elders.

The chaplain spoke about fear and the best, biggest, most important father of us all—God. To love God, one had to fear first! Getting older (not old), he explained, just gets you closer to your heavenly father waiting for you in heaven. I didn't find it particularly uplifting. It seemed rather strange for a Father's Day celebration called 'Summerfest'. Did he mean "Hallelujah, let's all die and get happy?" I surely don't want to get any older any too soon to find myself meeting up with that Maker!

The chaplain repeated the story about Sarah and Abraham. The Bible says that Sarah was 90 and Abraham 100 when they had a baby (this occurred BV—before Viagra). Who would want to be taking care of a baby at that age when you probably couldn't get out of bed to change a diaper—even if it was your own. I don't know what the good chaplain was suggesting to these folks. I think most nursing homes disapprove of residents having sex. Probably, it was more that Sara and Abraham were older and that life was still really good or something along those lines.

Our little trio played music right after that 'uplifting' sermon. We wore straw hats and long dresses to pull off the 'attitude' part. Anybody could tell we were old broads not chicks. I announced, "We dedicate our first song to Sarah and Abraham. It's called, 'Makin' Whoopee'." The other two chicks giggled. I'm not sure the residents heard me, but the minister did and grinned. The residents seemed to recognize the tune and clapped along.

Three Things

Keep these three things connected in your mind—trees, bananas and buckets; this is educational, I hope. First, I learned something new about holly trees—not that I ever knew that much about them in the first place. Our church has a small but quite beautiful memorial garden which has a beginning at the side of the front walk but needed a discernible end.

Naomi, one of our church's founders, has had a big part in planning the memorial garden of our Unitarian Universalist Church of the Shenandoah Valley. She suggested to the committee that perhaps if we couldn't afford to put a columbarium or a curved brick wall at the end of the garden, we could instead plant holly trees which would subtly and beautifully mark the garden's end boundary during all seasons.

The committee complied with her wishes and ordered several hollies to be planted. They arrived in due course, and hard-working church members planted them. Guess what? The hollies are deciduous. So, visit the garden when they have leaves and the garden is at its most beautiful, because that way, you'll know where it ends. That's all I have to say about deciduous holly trees. Oh, go ahead, keep reading. Here's some information on bananas which your mother never told you.

Here is how to peel a banana—thinking outside the box. Chimps do it this way, and it works for them. Peel the banana from the other end. Peeling from where the fruit held onto the rest of the stalk and tree is what we've all been taught. The right way to peel a banana is from the bottom end. The peel comes off so much more easily. Those stringy thingies also seem to let go with less effort. Chimps' actions speak louder than words. I promise they won't say, "I told you so." So, there you are—a lesson on peeling bananas, one more thing your mother never told you. Do try it.

Last but not least, speaking of what our mothers taught us, or didn't, my friend Judy is helping Naomi with some chores these days. Her mother instructed her on how to mop the kitchen floor. I guess most of our mothers taught us mopping either by design or osmosis. Judy puts water and whatever floor cleaner into the bucket just like the rest of us. Then, she sets the bucket into the sink. I'd never heard of attacking a dirty kitchen floor this way.

Naomi asked her why in the world she put the bucket into the sink.

Judy was somewhat flabbergasted. She responded with, "That's how my mother taught me to wash the floor!"

Naomi's next question was, "Why don't you put the bucket on the floor instead?"

"I don't want to kick the bucket."

Nobody does.

You do see how this last bit ties in with the first, don't you? The banana is the slippery part of the three little stories, but I couldn't think of another thing you didn't already know.

Hot Tomatoes in the Garden

I often introduce myself as Mark's trophy wife. Then, people remember who I am. If I come up with the usual handshake and "It's nice to see you," they move along rather quickly.

'Trophy wife' is another thing. Of course, they do a double take—one isn't married to one's 'trophy wife' for over 46 years now, is one? Wives and tomatoes—or rather trophy wives and hot tomatoes have something in common.

'Hot tomatoes' when I was young meant really cute or sexy women. Well, we've got two of them in our garden. Hot tomatoes, that is, not female hotties. They get all the attention the neighborhood has to bestow upon them. They started out as mere seedlings—cheap ones at that—but were painstakingly placed in the ground in the best possible soil mixture for this northwest corner of Virginia. Situated at the long legged light pole at the corner of our little plot of land, they are the only plants in the entire yard which get good sunlight. They also get ample rain in most years cooling them in the evening and feeding their growth by day.

So, what's the point? The point is that these two tomato plants look like the finest species ever developed by man or woman. They average four inches per day of new growth; they are sprouting healthy looking golden blossoms prematurely; their stems and leaves are cascading out and about the chicken wire cage constructed around them so as to be protected from menacing deer and groundhogs. So?

So, see the rest of the yard is just plain pathetic. Pretty purple cone flowers—approximately a dozen of them which should have been the showy species this summer—are headless and stunted. Camille sent me a dozen prize plants for Mother's Day. The groundhogs fancy their taste. I'll bet you didn't know that. Lilies are withering. Marigolds are holding their own but staying short and sticking close to the ground. Crab grass is giving the hot tomatoes a run for their money, but that genus always does well where I'm planted—especially with this latest rain.

In about a month, crowds of baby buggy pushers, skinny guy runners and kids on skateboards will stop and stare. They'll gawk and gaze in amazement at the extraordinary size of these hot tomatoes. For lousy plants, they get just about the same attention as those darn trophy wives get. What have they done to deserve all that? Stand there. Look pretty. Bend appropriately. Blossom profusely. Maybe flirt at the passing crowd. There you have it on some authority... mine! Trophy wives and hot tomatoes do have something in common.

Forever...Cookies!

Three large jars sit on the top shelf of a relatively unused space. We purchased them in one of those charming English villages full of 'shoppes'. Evidently, they started out as candy jars. Today, they store antique cookie cutters which once belonged to Mom and great Aunt Clara. Every imaginable kind of cookie cutter is represented except for movie characters and dinosaurs marketed in the past 50 years. Not only Christmas holidays but also Halloween, Thanksgiving and Easter cookie cutters can be found.

Did you also enjoy cookie making as a child? My mom began holiday baking the day after Thanksgiving and made at least one batch of cookies each day until Christmas arrived. Trays of delicious, decorated, colorful cookies were given to friends, the post office employees, and neighbors on both sides, across the street and behind us. Maybe the preacher got some too. Some cookies were works of art. When Doug and I had reached a responsible age, we were allowed to help roll out, cut and decorate.

Chris, Camille and I baked lots of cookies. I almost quit before I began when Chris was a baby. We lived in a little stucco house with a small back porch which served as cold storage. I didn't know about the sneaky Arlington squirrels who managed to open the tin tops and eat all the cookies stored in our outdoor containers. I imagine they were after the nuts, but they devoured all ingredients in the cookies. That may have been the year I got through the holidays without putting on extra pounds.

One year, we were lucky to have our niece Diane visit us for a couple of days with her six-year-old daughter Emmie just before Christmas. They baked cookies the last night they were here. These were cut and bake cookies where you slice a refrigerated roll into the number of cookies you want, plunk the slices onto the cookie sheet and stick them in the oven to bake.

Before baking, Emmie sprinkled green sugar—the only colored sugar I had on hand—on the top of the cookies. Diane allowed as how she wanted to keep the tradition alive in her family, but she was taking the easy way out. Emmie will remember baking cookies—they didn't have to come from scratch by creaming butter and sugar, adding eggs, then flour sifted together with baking powder. Her memory will be the taste of hot newly baked cookies straight from the oven just before bedtime. Diane, who hasn't forgotten her childhood, gave her a good, healthy chunk of cookie batter before they even began slicing.

Now, what will Emmie do with her children when Christmas rolls around and it is cookie cutting time? What will have taken the place of ready-to-bake cookie dough by that time? I'll bet something new will evolve. Maybe the next generation of moms will buy cookies and put them in the oven to warm up. When they emerge, they will smell just like freshly baked cookies which took hours to mix, refrigerate and cut. Remember, I have a couple hundred old antique cookie cutters if a cookie cutting rage returns. Don't forget to clean up the mess, because you will make one.

Sneaking Changes

My most recent turning point is life adjusting not life changing. "I've never seen anything like this!" exclaimed the podiatrist.

I thought I was taking him a rather common toe to look over. I've got a middle toe—which like a middle kid probably didn't get enough attention through life. It is growing. It has grown some extra skin and padding on its bottom, and now it is almost the size of my thumb.

Purchasing shoes these days costs more money than the down payment on my parents' first house. That means I can't be growing longer, fatter toes. I can't just afford to buy new shoes because a toe grows. My husband won't even look at it. He says if the podiatrist had never seen one, he didn't really want to either.

This life-adjusting turning point started a week after my 97-year-old mother died. She was the last of her generation. Yes, you know what that meant for me. I'm next. Maybe I have another 27 years to go if I'm going to live as long as Mom did. Mom lived with two artificial hips and one replacement knee, although she should have had two new knees.

In any case, I no sooner returned to Virginia after Mom's death than my knees stopped working. One locked. Both hurt. And, I thought, *what the heck is this? So, I'm next. But my knees don't have to be in such a hurry.* It turns out that the knee caps don't have cartilage. Maybe that toe padding got confused and ended up in the wrong part of my body. Thanks to magic knee goo, I can walk again without pain.

200

February brought GERD just before our vacation to South America. I won't go into all the gory details, but believe me, they are not pleasant. GERD means gastro-esophageal reflux disease; the symptoms are heartburn and indigestion. You'll recognize the dreaded GERD if you ever meet up with it.

Additionally, when nobody is looking, the tops of my hands sprout little broken blood vessels. I've never seen it happen. It's lightening fast. From one minute to the next, they'll appear. Many of my friends get this too. They say it's 'liver spots,' but I don't drink. Why would my liver spot otherwise?

This is all small stuff. To manage my new life, I've discovered Sam-E. It is a pill which makes one feel good even while the body falls apart. It's natural, over-the-counter and taken daily. I am able to deal with all these foibles with a sense of well being! Last night at a dinner party, someone told me it was herbal testosterone. Guess I'd better read the label. I'm not sure I need an additional malady.

I just need to be patient with these body parts which are rebelling because of our new age. I've gone off that testosterone business for good.

Bliss on the Internet

I was reminded again recently about bliss. You know how sometimes your whole being rises up feeling joyous? Sometimes it happens during a walk in the forest, watching a sunrise or sunset, receiving an unexpected phone call from a friend. Maybe this is a religious experience. Anyhow, I witnessed it again—quite by accident. Had I been a puppy, my tail would have been wagging furiously fast.

My cousin Nique had sent me a u-tube clip from Antwerp, Belgium. Julie Andrews' voice wafted over the train station waiting room, "Doe, a deer, a female deer, Ray a drop of golden sun," etc. Remember the song? One man, then joined by a woman, began to dance. It multiplied exponentially until the whole waiting area of the Antwerp Train Station was filled with people dancing—workers, students, travelers, all ages, many hues. Check it out by pasting this address into your browser.

http://www.youtube.com/watch?v=0UE3Cnu_rtY or

YouTube — Centraal Station Antwerpen gaat uit zijn dak!

Talk about a feel-good moment—an entire group of people in a waiting room dancing. The scene seems to be light years away from the usual hustle and bustle of a cold, impersonal, cavernous waiting room. This is a feel-good situation no matter who you are or where you come from. Yes, it was staged, but it is still wonderful.

I sent it onto many people, including Mark. Quite by accident, I passed his office as he was watching the video. Sitting back in his leather swivel chair with feet propped up on the desk, his whole relaxed body exuded a countenance of sublime happiness. His face had that special expression which I'm afraid I just can't describe. Written all over him is supreme contentment and joy all bound up together. The scene washed over me, and I'm sure he felt close to what I felt watching this u-tube.

Over four decades I've seen this in Mark many times. I'm overcome with love for him whenever it happens. These days, I'll often catch the look while he is absorbed in an opera. I saw it when I returned to Brasilia after a month in the states taking care of business. When he saw me enter the airport waiting room, he grinned from wrist to wrist. Joy—would that it were a daily occurrence for us all.

Today, I know he's feeling it. He's off on a mission in Washington, D.C. to research some American painters who are represented in Julian Wood Glass' art collection in the Museum of the Shenandoah Valley. It's a wonderful project for him. He loves learning like no one else I've ever known. Here's another educational opportunity, and it isn't about the political problems of the planet. I won't be able to watch his expressions while he researches today, but I know he'll come home with an interesting tidbit of some sort and be happy in its discovery.

Joyfulness! I'm going to will it to happen more frequently. I'll watch Mark more closely in the next few days to note the ways it happens. I was just thinking—I might even add to his quality of life.

Honey, Do

During our former life in the Foreign Service, we moved into a freshly painted house with each new tour. Often, we were overseas, but sometimes, we were in the states buying a place in which to live. Each place smelled like new paint.

Overseas I kept our homes looking as American as possible. As we were representing our country, I didn't go native with local furniture or décor. The public rooms were decorated with things from home. Over the years, people commented on how our home looked so American.

Unfortunately, it has been about 15 years since the living room of our retirement house here in Winchester was painted. The young family who lived here before us didn't do many improvements, cosmetic or otherwise. It is beginning to look a bit dingy; most of the downstairs is painted beige (or maybe they call it 'sand' or 'toast' or 'mocha'). Just before moving in on the first day of summer 11 years ago, we stripped the dining room of its wallpaper and painted it to match the living room.

Ruminating about painting the living room for the past few weeks has gotten me nowhere with Mark. He declares, "Leave it alone, it looks fine, why disrupt the whole house for a new coat of paint?" etc. I do understand his rationale. Why generate an additional mess unnecessarily? On the other hand, it is less of a mess than moving to another house freshly painted.

Then, I had an idea to move all our Foreign Service collections and paraphernalia up from the basement and down from the attic to decorate the living room. I proposed this idea to Mark. If he didn't like the idea of painting, we could change the ambiance of the downstairs. Think of all the good memories one could conjure up beginning with breakfast each day.

Mark turned ashen with this proposal. I guess it wasn't a good idea. Of course, it would entail too much work, and neither of us was looking for extra work. The next day I told him I agreed with him— we shouldn't and wouldn't be moving stuff up and down the stairs and around the house. I would, however, like to paint just the living room, dining room and hallway to freshen things up a bit.

"OK!" he chirped quickly.

Eureka! Compromise!

I called two painters and got estimates with a cost difference of $32. Tossing a coin, a painter was chosen. Paint was ordered, paid for, and it's done, finished in two days. All walls are now antique white—just like me.

Important Stuff

I have never been involved in the life of the mind. My mind hums along well enough for me to manage in the society I live in. I am interested in knowledge, but that always comes after my life of 'doing' is finished. Thus, I read books when it is too late, and then I fall asleep.

I have a special friend who spends the first two waking hours of each day reading the book she is reading. This is not a person without a full life. She is a performer, writer, teacher, gardener, dancer, traveler, daughter, mother, wife and friend to many. She gives time to all of the above. She travels a fair amount taking care of her elderly parents. She has decided reading is important to her, and she starts her day with a book.

It would drive me crazy to think I was taking time to read the beginning of each day. Probably that Protestant work ethic is hard wired. I do what has to be done before I allow myself the luxury of spending time as I wish. I love fiddling, weaving, writing and even e-mailing, but I just cannot entertain these passions before certain necessary jobs are finished. I was taught to get the unpleasant jobs over with first. I, of course, decide what is necessary and unpleasant.

Now, let us go back to the life of the mind. Four days in Wisconsin attending lectures at the convention my husband attended expanded my universe greatly. As you can see, I have not bought into a life of the mind yet or I would not be typing away at this dribble. I would be involved in serious pursuits of some kind—not unraveling my take on life. The lectures I attended were mind expanding.

A University of Wisconsin scientist discussed stem cell research. The possibilities seem without limit from drug discoveries to developmental biological studies to regenerative medicine.

Another scientist discussed how climate change in Wisconsin has been documented in various ways by various means. In the past 57 years, their growing season has increased almost a month on each end—in the spring and in the fall—due to faster thawing of winter and later freezing in the fall. This global warming lecture was specific to one particular area of our vast planet which made it local and easier to understand. It seems it is less cold in Wisconsin.

We visited the Niagara Escarpment, a larger geologic mass than the Grand Canyon itself. Additional field trips added to this week of the mind (as opposed to life of the mind). At least I got a week in!

The last lecture enveloped me completely. Given by Wisconsin's first poet laureate, once again, I got permission to write my story. Our stories are unique, although I already knew that. Our stories are the same as well. The poet laureate reiterated that we all experience owning, having, losing, courage, hope, healing, giving and receiving. Within these commonalities, we are each unique. We really do not begin to know ourselves until we write.

I learned our writing will fall somewhere between a grocery list and a Pulitzer Prize. Ms. Kort encouraged us all to write.

More Travels with Mark

Smiling sheepishly, Mark asked, "Do you want to ride down to Stephens City with me tomorrow?"

What? Tell me, have you ever in your life had an offer like that? After his having to fix his own lunch since I had made mine ten minutes earlier, the offer was made. My lunch was delicious by the way—cottage cheese and unsweetened applesauce—about a half cup of each, something under 200 calories for the whole business. He was thinking about a salad, but I knew none of the lettuce had been washed, and I didn't want to go there. (Sometimes retirement is like this).

I think he's getting hungry. Unsolicited luncheon and dinner invitations usually come about after an unusually dry period as far as creative, tasty, home-cooked food goes. We've got frozen fish in the freezer, but one gets tired of fish after several nights of it. So, I look forward to these respites from fish. When he gets hungry or bored with the fare, there's usually an invite in the works.

I was reminded how my dad used to offer the family a vacation in Eola. Eola was no more than a train stop between Naperville and Aurora. Stephens City has a whole lot more interest than Eola although it could use a passenger train.

Stephens City! What an opportunity. We go to church there each week. It is 12 miles south of town. It's not exactly a tourist destination although it has its charms.

Smiling, he looks as if he is offering me some grand opportunity like "Let's visit China!" Or, "What do you think about Patagonia in February?" This is a first for a Stephens City getaway. I can think of three great places to eat in Stephens City. Five exist, but I haven't tried the two newest places.

I turned him down. That in itself is unusual as I'm always in the market for lunch or dinner out. I have something more important to do today—pack for the longer trip we're making to Appleton, Wisconsin. We leave at six a.m. which means we'll have to be at BWI at four. Should we sleep or skip sleep entirely? We decide to sleep if possible.

Fast forward! Today's another day, another week, and another opportunity. We've 'done' Appleton and had a wonderful time. Arriving there in early morning felt like a trans-Atlantic flight. We hadn't slept much so didn't get much out of our first day there except a really good night's sleep that night. Returning home on another low-cost flight made our arrival back in Winchester in the very early morning, 2:00 a.m. Now, we've both recovered.

And, guess what? I've been asked for another date. He has forgotten he's been feeding me breakfast, lunch and dinner out for a whole week. We're going to the Museum of the Shenandoah Valley to eat lunch and to visit the photographic train exhibit. This will be followed by a fiddle practice for Little Noon Music this afternoon and "Man of La Mancha" tonight at the Wayside Theatre. Life is good—too good! How long can this last? I know that answer…as long as Mark loves entertainment. He is really into it! I'm the beneficiary!

Someday, I'll write about our travel after the Foreign Service since we moved to Winchester. We've done several Elderhostel trips, now newly named Road Scholar trips. In the United States, we've traveled to Hilton Head, Arizona, North Carolina (for humor!), Natchez and Lafayette (with a few days on our own in New Orleans), Delaware, St. Augustine and Fort Myers. In addition, we traveled across Canada on a train and spent a couple of weeks in Chile and Argentina. We visited Nova Scotia on a separate trip to hear fiddle music. By the way, it's a long way to Nova Scotia from Virginia by car. Our one Untour trip was to Eastern Europe—Prague, Vienna and Budapest.

We also traveled on our own for three weeks in Italy. Oh, yes, there was that fast, thrilling trip to China with a tour group. But, I'll leave all those stories for another time.

I'd like to travel to Croatia—Dubrovnik especially. Mark wants to go to Barcelona for a couple of weeks next spring. I'll go with him. We haven't been stay-at-home retirees yet. We're too busy spending the kids' inheritance.

An Embroidered Happy Life

We indeed attended a Wayside Theatre performance of "Man of La Mancha." After all these years, I believe that my mother-in-law (MIL) was truly a female Don Quixote. I grasped more of the story seeing it now than when I first saw it on Broadway when she treated us to the musical several decades ago. Maybe I'm now more familiar with inquisitions—or at least the human condition and coping with reality—or not.

Something about the play sparked my memory as I began thinking about MIL and my first encounter with her reality. It was that trip to Nyack to visit Mark's grandmother and her. I spent a few days with them before returning to Rio after seeing my family in Illinois. I remember standing in the bedroom overlooking the Hudson River. The telephone rang, and the call was for me. Mom and Dad were calling to tell me my Grandma Brian had died. MIL stayed in the room and kept pointing to the ducks on the Hudson in clear view from the bedroom window.

"Tell your mother about the ducks."

I covered the receiver with my hand and whispered, "My grandmother just died."

"Describe the ducks on the water which we can see right here through the window. The river looks lovely today."

I did it again, louder. "My grandma just died."

And so it went. She wouldn't hear me. She didn't want to deal with the reality. I was the new daughter-in-law (DIL), and our time together was to be perfect. I didn't know whether to laugh or cry.

Years before this incident, Mark's father told MIL he wanted a divorce because he had fallen in love with another woman. I understand she didn't scream at him, or ask him why or in any way emote about her grief, her rage, or the fact that single motherhood was being dumped upon her. Instead, she told him to go to the woman he loved. He did. Many years later, she recounted, "That night, the stars fell from the sky." Right. Poetic, isn't it? I would have reacted somewhat differently. Perhaps she assumed she would be that woman he would 'go to.'

She wore rosy-colored glasses. She embellished every situation to make it lovelier, more cheerful or charming. Even something unpleasant would be re-written or re-told so one wouldn't even recognize the original story. It wasn't easy for me to be around her for any length of time. She was in a different world—parallel maybe, but different. Sometimes I guess it's good to be disengaged from reality. I'm such a down-to-earth, pragmatic person. "I calls 'em as I sees 'em." Mark's grandmother never embroidered anything either—maybe MIL's perception of life was in reaction to too much practicality.

Tilting at windmills! The phrase is used to describe 'courses of action that are based on misinterpreted or misapplied romantic or idealistic justifications.' She was a master at re-working any situation. Although I do not believe in rebirth, I think she might have been the female reincarnation of Don Quixote living in 20th century America.

We've saved many of the letters she wrote us over the years. It will take some detective work to figure out what was really going on when she wrote them. The truth as others saw it was completely altered as she replayed events back to us. Hopefully, she had a blissful existence re-envisioning the world around her. I guess we all do that to some extent. She happened to be a master.

My grandmother died that day, the first of April in 1966, but I don't think my MIL, the psychiatric social worker, ever knew. Perhaps there was no way to idealize the event. I'm not sure why I'm writing about this incident. Maybe I'm still grappling with whether or not it is a good thing to live in the real world. Or did my MIL have the right idea of reinventing reality to suit her needs?

Clothes and This Mature Woman

I'd like to think about what women of a certain age are expected to wear these days. No, I'm not here to advocate for nudist colonies. And, I'm extremely grateful not to have lived 100 years ago with the fashions of that day. Coincidentally, my paternal grandmother was born on the very date I write this in 1888; she wore corsets and bustles; I'll bet she would have preferred loose and comfortable.

I've ascertained clothing for adult, grown-up women can be purchased only in the finest shops—those which advocate classic colors and styles, which have a certain tradition of color combinations and which look good on most people. Read high end.

A couple of years ago, I found a shop I enjoyed looking and shopping in. Their prices were fair, and they seemed to be reaching out to my demographic. I never left without at least a blouse. Looking for something springy and cheery, I returned about March—ready for winter to end. Everything in the shop, without exception, came in some shade of orange or purple. Neither color does much for this mature woman. Oh, yes, everything was fitted. Their marketing person must have been smoking something to veer that far off course. I guess I'd better take part of that sentence back. Parts of me are mature and pulpy, parts are worn out, and at least one part never got beyond 12 years of age.

Women like me are not looking for 'come-hither-look' clothing at our ages. We want something to make us appear somewhat stylish, perhaps svelte and not too frumpy. 'Age appropriate' is the correct term. Cotton and loose is my favorite style, but that doesn't always fit my persona either. Unfortunately, I've resorted to black, white and beige. Black is best for travel—nobody takes any notice of you. It doesn't show dirt too fast. Both beige and white go well enough with it.

Actually, I may have learned this many years ago while in the Foreign Service. Hijackings were rather commonplace, and we were told by security personnel always to wear drab colors when traveling by plane. That way, one wouldn't attract a hijacker's attention. Maybe my blah countenance and black-is-beautiful style should be blamed on the Foreign Service.

While in Italy a few years ago, Mark remarked on how I dressed just like those Italian women. Wow! What a compliment. He couldn't see the difference between those perfectly gorgeous creatures and his somewhat elderly wife? I thanked him for the compliment. He then asked, "How did you know all people here wore black all the time? You fit right in!"

For well over 46 years now, no matter what I wear or where we go, when we return home, he always says, "You were the prettiest girl there." Who cares about clothes?

The World of Tattoos

You tattoo too? Some of the classiest people I know have TATTOOS! One of them is my daughter who put her first lover's name prominently on her upper arm with a heart drawn around it. I guess she didn't realize then that first loves usually come and go. I haven't noticed any additional names added, so now she knows.

A leader in our community, a 30-year-old Latina dynamo with an eye toward political office, sports a small tattoo on her ankle. It doesn't look bad. So small and insignificant, I can't remember what it is. I wonder why she did it, because there must be some meaning behind it. Otherwise, it is hardly worth the pain she endured. One day I'll get down on me knees and check it out.

One of my adorable nieces has words written all around one wrist. They mean something like what my sister-in-law Rosemary once told me, "Life is about love or lessons".

A friend whose daughter got a tattoo decided to keep up with the younger generation and tattooed too. She showed us the tattoo one day—a large P on the top of her breast. She calls it her scarlet letter. The P stands for 'privileged'. I guess that makes a statement, but not too many people see it, I presume.

Another friend did the deed on her 50th birthday party. Since she is seeking the most meaningful Christian religion for her, it is a cross with the word "sojourner" underneath it. I guess the skin artist misspelled "sojourner" with the first try and had to add some additional stuff.

Although it has turned into a rather long arm tattoo, she is making a very appropriate statement, tattooed on her arm forevermore. She announced the other day that she had seen a perfectly beautiful bunch of broccoli tattoo recently. Do they go together?

Although there are bigger issues with which we should be concerned, it is interesting to me that Planet Earth has many humans with tattoos walking around everywhere. Those who cover every inch of skin with messages must be uncomfortable in their original skin.

A 72-year-old childhood friend of mine who began life looking good and wants to stay that way—continues to do so because of her frequent facelifts and botox injections. What price beauty? I guess that kind of thing isn't so important to me, because these days I'm more concerned about just putting one foot in front of the other and not tripping in the process.

I have recently learned facial tattooing is common in the Middle East. I observed lots of beautiful henna painting during our time living in Morocco—but that is North Africa, not the Middle East. Painted on hands and feet and rinsed into hair, I was not aware of other embellishments like tattooing.

So, tattoo away, world! Don't mind me. In case you think you weren't born with enough natural beauty, I guess it behooves you to add some. I will stick with what I got—some I got enough of, some I didn't, but I can't think what tattooed embellishments would do for me now.

A Noisy, Snowy Day

It was one of those days one longed for when one worked for a living—a frosty morning! Two inches of snow had fallen during the day yesterday. Evening dumped an icy frosting in the form of freezing rain. No traffic was moving on our roads this morning. Schools were closed. Ours and towns around us were shut down. Even the library didn't open—and that's when one needs a good book to read.

After a good solid breakfast of toast, a hard-boiled egg and two brimming mugs of strong black coffee, I headed back to bed. Yes, back to bed! Yesterday had been spent inside all day as I fought off some kind of stomach problem. To spend another full day at home seemed such a waste, and besides I was coming down with something unpleasant like a common cold, so back to bed I went at 9:30 to try to sleep it off. Yesterday's stomach problem had disappeared. So why not start the day with a nap?

So, back to bed I go. Mark closed the blinds because he thought it would be difficult to sleep again so soon after eight good hours of non-stop sleep. I didn't cover up. It seemed warm enough—quite cozy in fact. Radiators make the best heat. I no sooner closed my eyes than a rare sound interrupted my thoughts. It was a plane, coming closer. I didn't want to get up to watch, so I lay there just listening. It circled and disappeared. Then, it returned. Now, I was starting to wake up. I didn't want a plane landing on the house with me not yet dressed (for the photographers, you know).

Soon after 9/11 we had an Air Force jet circle our town in a false alarm when nerves were on edge and the powers-that-be thought someone was heading for the Capitol again. I didn't know why a plane would be this far out to intercept an intruder into Washington, D.C. airspace. It was unnerving to have a jet circling overhead during our outdoor market that Saturday morning. After all, we were 75 miles from the Capitol. This morning's sounds reminded me of that incident. Except it wasn't a jet. It wasn't loud enough to be a jet.

It did make enough noise to keep me from sleeping. Darn. Too many thoughts were interrupting my plans for a morning nap. Once you start thinking about 9/11, your mind wanders to all its ramifications—wars, threats, alienation from the rest of the world, a Presidential campaign, an election won, an Inauguration just over. No more sleep for me. I was wide awake now. So, I got up and decided to make the most of the day beginning with a third mug of strong coffee. That ought to do it.

Still in my nightclothes, (aka "soft" clothes), downstairs I paddled. I took another look outside at nothing moving. Even Mango the cat had gotten bored with his view from the radiator perch which looked out the front window. It seems that ice-covered snow had nothing slipping around it for the cat to enjoy from his special vantage point.

Then, the sound returned, but it was no longer high in the sky. It was right here outside the window. Snowplows were coming through! Who would have thought a snowplow and jet engine had anything in common? The snow and ice were being dislodged so traffic could move again. There were no planes being diverted or trying to land on icy runways after all. Now, if I could only get 9/11 out of my mind, I'd skip the coffee and try for another morning nap. They are delicious— morning naps. Coffee's not bad either.

Well, no, it is 10 a.m. now, time for Diane Rehm, and the coffee looks more inviting. I'll get another cup and start the day again. Life looks good again now that streets are plowed and we can get out for the Hepatitis A shots we need for our trip to Chile and Argentina.

Slow starting is sometimes a good thing. It makes you mindful of and grateful for snowplows—and even Hepatitis shots—the reason to get out of the house today.

A Lovely Old Lamp's Story

Maybe because my parents were frugal and held onto 'ancient' things, I have always loved old stuff. Because something had age, intrinsic value followed. That's not always so, but I have always wished antiques could talk. They have stories to tell, but alas, they have no memory or computer programs with which to write the stories. (I know, they lack other requirements for talking).

I remember my Aunt Marie telling Betty her daughter-in-law that my mom took exceptionally good care of everything she had. Had Mom lived with great privilege and many material possessions, she might not have taken such care with her worldly goods. I think about the glass-covered coffee table that Dad gave Mom for their first wedding anniversary. Under the glass went valentines, Christmas cards, get-well cards and all matter of doilies during the 73 years Mom cherished it. Of course, all three of us kids would have enjoyed extending its family history. Doug especially wanted to keep it and to protect family pictures under the glass.

Holes from a cherry pitter grace or mar—depending on your view—the top of our old French kitchen cupboard made of common wood for utilitarian purposes. Today, it holds electronic gear, which provides us with music and television in our little den off the living room. Where in France was the farm in which it was housed? Why did it leave the farm? To what uses was the locked top drawer put? A cherry pitter! Imagine. I've always managed to deal with cherry pits without a pitter. Obviously, the polite, classy French pit the cherries first! Of course, they pit for pies. They wouldn't spit pits.

Here is the reason I write about old stuff:

Last Thanksgiving when Mike and Karen made the trek to Virginia, they brought along 'the lamp' which once had been a kerosene lamp in a tavern in Plainfield. Early in the 1950s it moved to the front hallway of our house on Lockport Street.

The lamp left Plainfield along with Mom and Dad when they moved to Naperville.. This lamp has had many magic moments over its lifetime. I guess one can't say that lamps have lives, but this one at least has had an illustrious career. Still surrounded with its original opaque glass shade, now over a hundred years later, it has left Illinois. Today it is adjusting to Virginia and a continuing family saga. I hope that it will hear good stories from the folks at our dining room table— the same table it hung above in Illinois—and that it will grace the home of Brian descendants for many more decades.

When Mom broke up housekeeping and could no longer move the lamp from one apartment to another, she told me that she wanted me to have both her trivets (a story for another time) and the lamp. I would cherish all. I grew up with all of them. Then, on a visit to see us here in Winchester, Mom told me that Doug (who, of course, also grew up with the lamp) wanted it too. Doug was one of her caretakers and had been for many years, so I did not hesitate for a moment in saying, "Doug should have the lamp!"

He and his wife, Judy, had no place to hang the lamp, so Judy sent it on to Winchester with Mike and Karen this year.

Since Mike also has many fond memories of the lamp, he will inherit it from me. He and I made a plan to keep this special artifact in the family. We'll behave as aristocrats do and pass it on through the generations. After Mike's demise, it will move on to the oldest grandchild. It will be up to the grandchildren either to enjoy the lamp or to pass it on to the next in line. After Michelle, the youngest grandchild, has her time with the lamp, she will pass it on to the great grandchildren. Unfortunately, I will not be around to orchestrate these moves. I'll leave instructions. Somebody else will have to inform the other great grandchildren who come along. So far, there are three great-grandchildren in the line of inheritance. There will many more.

The lamp brings light along with so many happy memories. In the great scheme of things, the lamp is not important. However, it has been a symbol of our family's life together, and I'll cherish and care for it during mine.

I believe that is enough about magic old stuff. Now, all we have to do is to stop fighting wars, curtail global warming, feed the multitudes, house the homeless, fight disease and eliminate wanton killers and weapons of mass destruction.

The caretaking order as of today is after me, Mike, Chris, Tricia, Camille, David, Rachael, Michelle, Dara, James, Raeanna and future descendents yet unborn. Until then, we'll take good care of it.

Real Magic Moments

Have you experienced unexpected magic moments? I want you to know about these extraordinary events in my life. Maybe they shouldn't take on such great importance, but I'm heartened by the humanity of each story.

Not long ago, I fiddled for the demented folks at Harbor Place in the nursing home where Mom was living. People called this section of the building a 'safe place'—a harbor. The occupants were suffering from some kind of dementia, and the door had to be locked because some of them 'walked.'

Mom was obviously delighted I had come with fiddle. She sat in a seat toward the front where she could see everything and grinned nonstop. Everybody seemed cheerful. Maybe dementia fools people into thinking they're happy, or maybe they are. It couldn't be that they all loved violin music.

Guitar-playing Michael, (a former boyfriend of my niece Rachael), and I had volunteered to provide some musical entertainment for the residents on that Saturday afternoon. A few months earlier, I had learned when people are suffering from dementia, the most you can do for them is to provide *moments* of pleasure.

We started with the bluegrass tune 'Old Joe Clark.' Imagine my surprise when we played through the tune a dozen times because Jimmie, a stately black woman of questionable age, catapulted herself into the song and belted out every known verse with unbridled gusto.

Others tapped out the rhythm. I'm quite sure my face didn't hide my amazement at Jimmie's prowess with all the words to the tune. Michael and I carried on over and over and over again.

Her singing all verses of 'Old Joe Clark,' was a magic moment for me. Tears welled up in my eyes as I watched and listened to her sing. Her long-term memory had returned to being a sharecropper's daughter and remembering the words to a song she sang long ago.

Every morning for over five years, Jimmie had asked the attendants where she is and how long she has been there. She may have no idea of her surroundings, but in addition to her uncanny ability to remember all those lyrics, she has been crocheting complicated patterns all that time. Compared to other residents' rooms, hers is wild with rainbow colors of doilies and scarves.

Jimmie's singing made most of us euphoric, but a petite woman, Regina, just watched the performance and didn't applaud at its end. When the song finally ended, Regina leaned over to Michael and me and whispered the only thing she could say in English, "I'm an Italian girl." Michael beamed.

He countered with "I'm an Italian boy," and proceeded to serenade her with *That's Amore*. Then, she couldn't stop smiling. Hollywood's central casting could not have pulled it off any better. Tears rolled down my cheeks. It was a magic moment of happiness for the 'Italian girl' and for Michael and me too. In that brief instant, all was right with the world. There we were trying to give people a few moments of pleasure, and we left with memories for a lifetime.

A third unexpected situation happened a few weeks later when my husband and I vacationed in Natchez. We learned from hotel personnel there were no coin-operated laundries in town, so on a dismal, rainy afternoon, we drove to the other side of the Mississippi River to Vadalia, Louisiana, to wash a week's worth of dirty clothes.

We found 'Mom's Washateria' on a pothole filled highway located in a dreary, almost abandoned, strip mall. A sense of desperation permeated the place. The dimly lit notices on the walls gave information about having your baby, getting onto Medicaid or joining the Army. This place felt darker and dingier than most laundries I remember.

The pouring rain added to the depressing scene. But, wait…

The attendant converted our dollars into change without a problem. After sorting clothes and getting them loaded into the quarter-eating machines, I moved over to the other side of the room to wait.

I was interrupted by a pretty, perky 'twenty-something' woman sprouting cornrows, all dressed in pink jeans and matching jacket who sauntered over to where we were sitting. Smiling broadly, she handed me a bunch of quarters. "Here, you'll need these."

Startled, I looked up at her and asked, "Why are you giving me this money?"

"You'll need it!" *Did her morning horoscope tell her to look for a needy woman today?* Although I tried to give the money back, she insisted I keep it.

After she left, I asked the attendant what that was all about, and she responded, "Some people think it will bring them good luck to give money to strangers."

I hope this generous young woman did indeed have good luck that grey day. I passed the money onto the next 'washer woman' to enter the laundry. She smiled broadly and said "THANKS!" Aha! Maybe this is a local custom.

We drove back to Natchez, and in spite of the dull rainy day, the warm fuzzy feeling stayed with me the whole evening. I learned an important lesson from that young woman. Maybe instead of folks asking for a handout, a new mantra might be taking hold—a new meaning to "give and you shall receive."

These three magic moments took place where life often looks particularly dreary—in the dementia unit of a nursing home and in a scruffy coin-operated laundry. Just think of the powerful moments we must be missing in bright sunlight.

Here We Are

Do you remember that Winston Churchill once said "You make a life by what you give."

Dad often told me, "In the scheme of things, in another 50 or 100 years, this won't make any difference." He was usually referring to some insignificant occurrence in my life which I probably thought was nothing short of earth shattering.

Speaking of the earth, looking at the heavens the other night at a Virginia state park along with hundreds of others, our place in the scheme of things all seemed to shake out and make some sense. As the universe is just too big for me to fathom, my solution is to come down to the nitty gritty of the lives we as individuals live.

In a nutshell, we are born and then we die. Because dying is a certainty and because we have reasoning power which other animals don't possess, we spend vast amounts of time in a search of a meaning for our existence. Over the millennia millions have killed countless other millions because their belief systems differed.

I am exceedingly grateful for the gift of life itself. That egg and that sperm united to make me. What a chance we take on just becoming! Think about it: what are the chances of our just being born? My finite brain can't get around that! Think of all the others there might have been—but instead, here I am! And, there you are.

I'm still not certain about my reason for being, so I don't worry about the question of heaven and hell. What I've found to be possible is to connect to the greatest degree possible with others inhabiting the planet with me—my fellow travelers—my family, friends, neighbors, acquaintances, community and many people whom I'll never meet.

A popular radio psychologist thirty years ago 'told me' that life wasn't a dress rehearsal. Although already aware of that, from then on, I've tried very hard to prioritize carefully my life's activities—from raising my children to be responsible adults who contribute to the greater good to deciding which non-profit can best use my monetary contributions to improve lives of others.

Today is the celebration of Martin Luther King's life. Because of him and many others like him, social justice is very high on my list of priorities—and although race relations are not as bad as they once were, there's still much to be done to equal the playing field for people of color. The latest marginalized group is homosexuals. Where do we begin in righting these wrongs? In our families, churches, neighborhoods, state, country? Homosexuals don't have the same civil rights that we heterosexuals have just because of who they are. Frightening, isn't it?

It is all very simple really—it's about 'walking a mile in someone else's moccasins.' How about the golden rule which is found in all world religions? Where does discrimination against anyone get us? Higher on the pecking order, I know. Speaking of pecking order, that reminds me again of that egg. I am so grateful for life itself and am enjoying my journey immensely. I hope you are too!

I think Winston Churchill was right when he said, "You make a life by what you give." And so was Martin Luther King. And so are all the others working to alleviate some of the glaring inequities of the planet's people.

Losing Greats

They all left us in the same week—Cronkite, McCourt and Holland. And so, where do I begin? Of course, I had 'known' Walter Cronkite the longest. With our being in and out of the country over the years, he wasn't a constant presence in our living room each evening. However, I especially remember his news coverage during the Viet Nam war. One evening, he talked about his 12-year-old son whom he didn't want fighting this war when he came of fighting age. I didn't think wars lasted such a long time. Now I know differently. Being a news junkie most of my life, I feel I've lost a friend with Walter Cronkite's passing. We in the viewing public trusted him, his honesty and his judgment. Newsreaders don't necessarily transmit those feelings to us these days.

Soon after reading Frank McCourt's book *Angela's Ashes*, I took a workshop on memoir writing. The book was top on the list as a memoir not to miss. It was more than a memoir, however. It was about abject poverty and what that involves. It was beyond anything my imagination could have ever constructed. I hope the book stays in the literature forever. These kinds of living conditions for human beings should not be tolerated anywhere in the world. Somehow or another Frank McCourt and those siblings who lived made it through the muck. For a high school English teacher, he left quite an inheritance for us all.

Then there's Jerry Holland. What a fiddler he was! I didn't know him until the summer we traveled to Nova Scotia. We went to hear live fiddle music but were never in the right place at the right time. We heard lots of recorded music wherever we went, and that was a great plus—it was always the best Cape Breton fiddle music played over loud speakers. I bought a music book by Jerry Holland at the Gaelic College of Celtic Arts and Crafts. I got home to Virginia and realized there wasn't much I could play from it.

I got the book out again a few days ago after Jerry's death and played all the songs he had written. Only in his early 50s, he died after a long bout with cancer. What a loss. I'm so grateful to have this fine book. My favorite tune is "My Cape Breton Home" which Jerry wrote for his dad (also a fiddle player) many years ago. It is a very beautiful air.

They say we can't grieve for the people who die with whom we have no personal relationship. That is not true. These three have left legacies for us. I along with millions of others will grieve their passing. As a news junkie, wannabe writer and wannabe fiddler, I am grateful to all three for enriching my life as they did. I hope they realized the enormous contributions they gave millions of us. Wouldn't it be wonderful if we could all leave legacies of such import? We'll all do what we can, won't we?

Ordinary Things

The house of friends of ours blew up. The explosion was heard for miles around. Carol knew everything was destroyed, but she sifted through the rubble anyhow. She finally found a letter opener from their first tour in South America. Now, that letter opener has become precious. No one was in the home at the time of the explosion, so there was no loss of life. The authorities determined it was a gas explosion. A new furnace had been recently installed, poorly.

This explosion is not as horrific as tsunamis and earthquakes which take lives in the hundreds of thousands and destroy everything forever. It does represent to me how much is lost of things we hold dear—letters, photographs, everyday, unimportant stuff with no intrinsic value but precious nevertheless.

I will not write a story about Mom's black plastic combs. It's enough to say that after her death when my brother Mike and his wife Karen and I went through the few possessions in her space in the nursing home, we gave most things away. For some reason, I held onto her combs. They had combed through her hair, and it would be a way to stay attached to Mom to have her combs sit on my dresser.

You can imagine what our home must house if I hold onto things like combs. It's not the dollar value that makes them cherished. Quilts! I don't have that many, but one pink and white one was made for my parents' wedding gift in 1932 by my great Aunt Clara. Another blue and white Irish chain quilt was made by Margaret Almira Milligan, my great-grandmother who died when Grandpa was only nine. A square made from my maternal grandmother's thread bare quilt hangs on the wall to my left, always reminding me of where I've come from.

Also, there's Dad's turquoise glass drinking cup. And, the fabulous watercolor fish Chris painted in kindergarten and the pen and ink dog drawing done by Camille in third grade and on it goes. Stuff can represent so much.

Home

I've been thinking about how home can mean both a place and a state of mind. Sometimes we have both. The homeless often say they wouldn't want the burden of a home—too much to care for, too much responsibility, too costly. To the person whose home is a place, it is difficult to understand a homeless person's being content not having that place. If I don't have a home, I'm looking for one.

We lived in several places during my childhood. The home I remember with great fondness was the big old white wooden house with bay windows, front and back stairways and a wonderful front porch the width of the house. Fifteen wooden trunks and newspapers from the Civil War were uncovered in the ancient barn behind the house. Big trees lined the street. It was Plainfield, Illinois, during my formative years. For a teenager, life was good and so simple then. Looking back with selective memory, it was 'perfect.' I was part of a larger community and lived in a safe, supportive cocoon with Mom, Dad and my two brothers.

After marriage in 1964 and short stays in Laurel, Maryland, Rio de Janeiro and Brasilia, Brazil, Luanda, Angola and Rabat, Morocco, fast forward to nine years into the Foreign Service (1974), where Mark and I found ourselves living at Avenue Capitaine Piret, 63 where a gentle, sloping street of ornamental cherry trees set the stage for the half-century old townhouses in Brussels, Belgium. Walled gardens viewed from the back veranda were beautiful. This was a home and state of mind combination our whole family enjoyed for three years.

Quality of life was of utmost importance to Belgians, and we Americans learned a thing or two about it. Cultivating some European habits was a most enjoyable challenge. We shopped daily for fresh food for that evening's meal. Belgians boast of consuming both the best chocolate and coffee in the world.

These are homes where that illusive state of mind played a part. Our homes were comfortable, a refuge from the world beyond but also included that special component—which was ours for the making. Maybe others living in those homes might not have had the same feelings about them.

We begin our 11th year here on Courtfield Avenue in Winchester come the first day of summer. We've never lived anywhere for such a long time! This simple 'American four-square' house must be in alignment with the planets as we course through time and space as it has become home and a state of mind for both Mark and me.

It feels like coming full circle as living in Winchester can be almost like returning to the 50s in northern Illinois. As the Apple Blossom festivities took place, I felt myself in a time warp of sorts and flitted between childhood memories and the weekend's realities of fire engines roaring by, fireworks interrupting the quiet of the night and friends and family arriving Saturday for food, fellowship and the Grand Feature parade.

Seasons

Do you have a favorite season? Spring and fresh air go together in my mind, so I think I would say spring is my favorite. On *Avenue Capitaine Piret* in Brussels, ornamental cherry trees bloomed in great profusion on both sides of the whole length of the avenue. On a sunny day, nothing in the world could look more delicious. It was indeed a vitamin pill for the soul.

Portugal and Belgium's muted seasons could bring winter rain and bone-chilling dampness. Sometimes in Rio's winter, it rained cool. In the tropics, most outpourings from the sky added more heat and humidity to the already hot, muggy, still environment. Let's return to spring as we know and love it.

Spring brings new green growth on trees and in grass, brief beautiful showers, and bright, jewel-colored crocus bravely breaking ground even with possible snow in the offing. Fresh air! Re-birth! Each year, spring is my favorite season, and then after summer, autumn arrives. How could one chose between spring and autumn? Both seasons delight all my senses. Although my least favorite season, summer, has its good points, especially if you love the heat.

Sounds and smells of summer take me back to my childhood. I've lived through many summers, but I remember most fondly those of my childhood. I remember the smell of new mown grass, the cool taste of lemonade and endless time spent in doing absolutely nothing. Events and non-events announced summer's arrival.

Scents of fresh growth and sometimes manure filled the air wafting around town in all directions. Everybody cut the grass using hand mowers propelled by human beings pushing them. The unique purr could be heard from all directions. The noise didn't pollute the neighborhood. With push mowers, you didn't infringe on anyone else's peaceful environment. The sound was pleasant, comforting, and steady.

Ice-cold lemonade sold from hastily built stands was a common occurrence. Being young entrepreneurs, Doug and I also wove potholders on square steel looms with sock tops and sold them cheap—two for a quarter—when you also bought some of our lemonade. All sorts of make-believe animals appeared in the puffy clouds overhead. Ah—to be a kid again!

Sounds of children playing—kick the can, hide and seek, the crack of the bat, hopscotch—took place all over town. You heard kids giggling their delight or sometimes wailing to a parent, "Mommm, he hit me again!" Do you ever hear those sounds anymore?

I hardly hear kids outdoors these days. Maybe they learned the adage, "Children should be seen and not heard." More likely, they are inside clicking at a machine for entertainment. OK, I will give them the benefit of the doubt—perhaps air conditioning sounds drown out outdoors' sounds. There were no air-conditioners when I was a kid.

The cacophony of summer sound was all over town. Organ music emanated from the skating rink down near the tracks on the west side. Everybody skated to those Second World War vintage tunes. I was a wimp even then and only skated with someone else to keep me upright. I had many sore black and blue knees to prove my ineptness (mind you, there were only two bad knees at a time!) Remember, this was the only entertainment in town outside the movie theater. I was ever so much better at sitting in a dark theatre watching cowboys and Indians carry on.

Fall brings a nip in the air and the scent of fallen leaves, sometimes burning. All colors mix in a dusty mélange promising simmering sounds and smells of stew on cold winter days. When I was a kid, we all loved raking. I don't remember growing blisters while raking as a kid. Maybe it wasn't a chore then but just part of the program. Leaves fall. In our culture, one rakes them up. In the 'olden days,' one also lit bonfires and roasted marshmallows in the shooting flames. Marshmallows, with their well burnt and crispy outsides and gooey, sticky and oh-so-sweet insides, added greatly to the smell and taste of autumn. Ah! And, don't forget s'mores!

I remember jumping into piles of leaves. What I don't remember is ever bumping into the scent or encountering any dog poop at the bottom. We'd rake the leaves up high and jump into the pile again. Did we worry about the dust from the dried earth and dirty leaves? I don't think so! After all, we took baths and washed our hair on Saturday nights to be ready and clean for church on Sunday.

Even with global warming, I hope winter will always roll around in northern Illinois. In mid-winter during the Christmas season, everybody went caroling to brighten the season for shut-ins and the elderly. Often treated to hot chocolate, we were always invited inside so everyone could hear our dulcet sounds better and so the warm air couldn't rush out the open doors. Cookies, as payment for services rendered, seem to me to be an outstanding idea to this day. These were my good old days!

In our small town mail was delivered to the Post Office boxes twice a day, so when carrying on a long-distance romance, corresponding with my Scottish pen pal, or hoping for a Christmas card from the latest beau, at least during Christmas holidays, I'd trudge the distance twice a day—in snow, sleet, rain—you name it.

Speaking of snow, new fallen snow was a delight! We could eat it, make angels in it and make snowmen and igloos and snowballs with it. We had more than our fair share of snow in northern Illinois, and we played in it all winter. Yes, we felt the cold! The river froze, and we skated on it. We did lots of sledding on the few hills in Plainfield. Frostbitten noses were an everyday occurrence then. When it wasn't snowing, the sun shone brightly on those crisp, cold winter days. People who live in cold climes capitalize on their good fortune and make the weather and what it dumps part of their joy of living. I know I wouldn't love winter, ice, snow or wind so much at my age now.

However, winter produced a perfect playground for a kid.

We were alive in our environment. Our entertainment was self-made. We didn't sit in front of television sets probably because we didn't have them yet. Yes, our senses too were alive! We smelled, saw, heard, felt and tasted the world around us. It was a wonderful way to spend one's childhood.

Liz and the Bigot

Years ago, when Elizabeth Taylor was married to Virginia's Senator John Warner, she told me (and you too if you were listening) that elastic waistbands were not doing women any favors. Actually, they were a curse, because they allowed too much flexibility.

Elizabeth and I have had a few things in common. I didn't get into the sequential monogamy thing she did. (You do remember what the sixth husband said? He was nervous about their wedding night because he knew what to do but wondered how to make it interesting).

Back to waistbands. I wore elastic waistbands, because I had quit smoking. In addition, I was getting older, and a middle age spread surfaced. About this same time, a sister-in-law sent me "White Diamonds" perfume for Christmas. It was Liz' brand, and on the tag Rosemary wrote, "Don't we all want to smell like Elizabeth Taylor?" I'd never thought about that before but decided, "Well, yes!"

I loved the scent and when I ran out, I bought some more. I not only was getting older like Liz but smelled the same. Recently, I've developed allergies to perfumes. However, in spite of it all I'm back thinking about Liz, because I'm wearing new slacks with a waistband rather than elastic. We may not smell the same any longer but we both wear waistbands. OK, the similarity ends there.

Another famous personality who influenced me was none other than Archie Bunker. You haven't noticed, because you're not around in the mornings, but I have taken some advice from Archie the bigot played by Carroll O'Connor. Do you remember him from the TV show "All in the Family," the show without any political correctness whatsoever? He was always picking on his son-in-law whom he called Meathead and I can't remember what else. I think of the both of them every morning—the bigot and Meathead.

On one totally improvised episode, Archie was telling Meathead how to put on shoes and socks. The son-in-law was putting on one sock and then the shoe, followed by the other sock and the other shoe. Archie shrieked at him that he wouldn't be able to run in case of a fire. He should put on one sock and then the second—one shoe and then the other—that way he'd be balanced to depart quickly if need be.

I'll bet Carroll O'Connor (if he were still alive) and Elizabeth Taylor would be pleased to know what an impact they've had on my life. So far, the shoe and sock bit is working just fine. However, there is one downfall to waistbands with zippers and buttons. One needs to think way ahead before a visit to the ladies room. It's not just a tug on the elastic pants anymore. You get my drift? The pants take more time now. So, here I am in my golden years no longer smelling like the white diamond Elizabeth Taylor is. But, I'll bet she has to do some advance planning too! And, in case of fire early in the morning while the shoes and socks are going on, I can now run with the meatheads!

Moku Yoku

During my walk this morning, I tried 'bathing under the trees.' It is called *moku yoku* in Japanese—*moku* means tree, and *yoku* means shower with water. It's a peaceful, calming, soothing activity. One listens to the "heartbeat of the trees," the rhythm of gentle swishing sounds of wind rustling leaves overhead. With enough surrounding silence, one can indeed hear it. What a lovely concept. How Japanese!

This morning, I concentrated on the sounds around and above me as I wandered through our neighborhood. The ipod stayed at home in a drawer. Instead of the most recent news, I concentrated on being alive. What a revelation! Although miles away, the white background noise of I-81 never left. It looks like I must forever live in last century's technological marvels which discharge noise. I could hear the steadfast reverberations of people driving to places and moving goods—all busy doing. I learned that at least today, birds were far noisier than trees. Even with the highway racket, their cheerful songs added joy to the ambiance. Although unseen, their music charmed!

Unfortunately, in our neighborhood, band saws are busy building bigger homes and additional outdoor living spaces. From all directions, their encroaching sounds disturbed what might have been a quiet space. I tried to ignore the din and listened instead to untold numbers of birds warbling their varied tunes. With amplification, it would have been such a cacophony of bird calls! What are they up to? Are they singing about the joy of being alive or are they calling for a mate? Are they chatting about the best local bird feeders? Or, are they just being birds?

A butterfly flitted across my path leaving just its shadow as it passed by. I liked seeing a butterfly so early in the morning and then wondered how and when they slept. Were they early risers? Were they into early morning exercise too? I'd never thought about their habits before. Overhead a jet soared across the cloudless sky. Unfortunately, those folks on board weren't listening to birds or bathing in the woods but instead heard engine noise and captains talking while chomping on peanuts for breakfast. Maybe they will listen to the birds and be inundated by trees another time.

On returning home, unwilling to leave this tranquility, I perched myself onto the porch swing for awhile to take in the sweet early morning sunlight at my back. Tomorrow, I'll set off to bathe again and perhaps once more meet up with the cricket who welcomed me home today. I was delighted to learn they aren't all in our basement.

Now, I'll return to reality and a shower with wet water to begin my regular day. Stay tuned. I'm learning about voluntary simplicity. I'm happy to learn about bathing under the trees. In the rainy season, it could save on water bills, don't you know?

Tarnish on the Golden Years?

Frozen chicken breasts were just the ticket this morning after the long walk up and down Winchester's western ridge. After concluding the walk, I decided to emulate my cousin's husband Earl who ices down his bad knee after running. I walk don't run. (Don't you remember your parents admonishing you to "walk, don't run"?)

I've never been a runner and even my slow walking has some negatives—especially because of the hills one encounters in our neighborhood. Nevertheless, the slow-walking knees love the coolness of the frozen breasts after scuttling over arduous hills which they never contracted to undertake. I didn't ask the knees and hips whether or not they wanted to walk this morning. In all honesty one shouldn't be caught discussing exercise with one's body parts, should one?

Everyone knows some people do grow old and reach their golden years. Most people understand we are all headed down the same path if we're lucky. Our resident pen pal chemist has reminded us that gold doesn't tarnish, but the 'years' in 'golden years' sometimes lack luster.

I hadn't expected to arrive at those golden years any time soon. After a hysterectomy at a relatively young age, I figured physical troubles were over for the long haul. Unfortunately, there are other body parts not removed with the hysterectomy. In addition to the root canals all dentists wanted to perform at one end of my body, foot doctors got into the act at the other end because of feet abused by high heels. I hadn't figured on feet going bad. I hadn't figured much of anything at all. Who plans for the golden years outside of having the financial means to 'survive' them? This is not to say that tarnish on the golden years doesn't exist. Many diseases loom for the elderly no matter how much dancing, crossword puzzles or fiddling one does to hold those maladies at bay.

Employing mind over matter, I have developed a little daily respite from aches and pains which takes place before four each afternoon. With the last cup of coffee of the day, I eat an apple. It may be an ordinary apple, but it is embellished. It is dipped into a mixture of equal parts low fat yogurt and peanut better. Sometimes, I imagine I'm eating cheesecake, sometimes a candied apple or a slice of German apple strudel. Sometimes, I pretend I'm sitting outside a charming Paris café with busy Parisian pedestrians heading hither and yon.

So, you see, in addition to reducing pain of aching knees with frozen chicken breasts in the morning, I'm feeding my psyche and wanderlust each afternoon with a delectable treat. It comes close to a religious experience, and I'm able to carry on the rest of the day with dinner preparations and evening activities. What's not to love about this? Tarnished golden years exist. But I ignore the situation for a few moments each afternoon with this little pleasure. Down with tarnish! Up with imaginative thinking!

In and Out of Shadows

Shadows surround us. Long, short, dark, muted, old or new, they are with us.

Some are welcome in the heat of day. We make some. Whether we like it or not, we exist in the shadows of those who lived before us as well as contemporaries casting them currently. Some are so sad.

As children we were sometimes reprimanded for questionable behavior by shadows of some who came before, as in "Your grandmother would have been appalled." Even after their deaths, our forbearers' characters lived on casting shadows onto future generations. Maybe the expression 'turning over in his grave' is the same thing as casting your shadow after death. One might surmise from this that it's a good thing to tell your stories if you want to cast shadows on future generations. Then, we might someday turn over in our own graves! Now, that gives new definition to 'shake, rattle and roll,' doesn't it?

There are many ways to shadow. One might be to keep a child from becoming what he might be by casting a shadow over him and his ambitions—filling him with self-doubt or leading him in a different direction from his heart's desires. At the other extreme, often the stage mother steps into the limelight and inadvertently shadows her child from center stage. After all, it was she who produced that kid. How about emulating one whom you admire—shadowing him or her? I used to 'shadow' experienced docents at the Glen Burnie historic house to note how they gave tours before I started giving my own.

Our founding fathers cast enduring shadows in crafting our democracy 'of the people, by the people and for the people.' Although we abide by their words even today, we debate, manipulate and massage meanings to make the Constitution live for the current generation. One does not manipulate shadows easily.

Shadows are good or bad depending on the eye of the beholder, aren't they? I'm grateful for those left by my ancestors. It gives me a clue into their psyches. "No Brian girl has ever been divorced," was one of my Great Aunt Clara's cautions. She didn't stop to think that daily thrashings by a husband might have been reason to divorce. Knowing Aunt Clara as I did, it may not have entered her mind that a husband would beat his wife. After all, one marries for love.

In my home, memories of loved ones, as well as inanimate stuff, cast shadows daily. I have lots of both. Let's just glance into the basement where my "modern" doll house is stored. After outgrowing the home-made wooden red one crafted by my dad, I moved up to a suburban kind of tin painted doll house. I look at it all folded up, situated in its box, and memories flood over me. It's a wonder I get anything done at all when I venture to the basement. The chunky, white kitchen appliances were obviously hand made, for the home made doll house, perhaps by my naughty grandfather. Shadows almost bowl me over thinking about him—the good and the bad. Then, there's a box full of pink plastic furniture and walnut grained plastic dining room table and chairs, obviously upscale for the time. Mom made sofas and chairs of cardboard and covered them with fabric. That furniture was for the modern, tin house. Ah! Memories!

Also in the basement are decades old Christmas ornaments and decorations—made by or given to us by people precious to our family. Shadows? My dad's loom! My $10 hutch purchased for our first home. Everywhere I look—there are shadows. Don't worry—I'll spare you from looking upstairs. The attic would knock you over.

Shadows are everywhere—reminding us, teaching us, shading us. We might as well get used to working out the way one deals with one's shadows. How do we benefit from them? How do we incorporate them into our lives? How do we construct our own to enlighten the next generation?

Old shadows can educate us in our daily lives by giving us guidance from others—dead or alive. Perhaps the shadows we create can enlighten future generations. What an opportunity! What an obligation! Maybe I'd better hang out in broad sunlight or at a minimum watch how and where my shadows might fall. I must be responsible.

Death Happens...

Although it reflects life, looking in the mirror, often reminds me of death. I see my Auntie Bum! Only 17 years older than I, people often took us for sisters. I don't know how we inherited this shared 'look'. We never could find ourselves in our ancestors' photographs. She was Dad's only sibling and one of my favorite aunts. I was told she couldn't pronounce her name, Bernadine, as a little girl. It came out sounding like Bumble Bee, and by the time I came along, it was shortened to Bum.

Being reminded of her when I look in the mirror is somehow comforting. It ties us together. She died four years ago on the first day of summer. I will always miss her. Her daughter, my cousin Nique, has told me she often catches her mom's expressions on my face.

Auntie Bum left us a long time before her death. She suffered from dementia and checked out before her physical death when her heart stopped beating. Following in her footsteps was my mother, born 11 years before Auntie Bum. Mom, at 97, had little memory of the almost century of life she had lived.

One time, my dad asked me to consider, "Do we mourn someone's loss because they have died? Or do we mourn others' deaths because of the effect on us?"

More than my future demise, I think about losing my friends and family. They're such an integral part of my life. When I check out, I'm gone, but when they check out, I'm left bereft. I've been left so many times recently.

247

It just isn't easy being a player in this evolutionary process—being born and then dying—when the living goes by so fast. I realize dealing with loss is a 'normal' part of life and aging. Adjusting to loss is so difficult. We lose our aunts and uncles; our mom couldn't remember us; my brother and close friends pass away while still quite young.

And, then I shake myself a bit and think about the odds of being born in the first place. Are we not the lucky ones? We were all given LIFE. What are the chances of our being born anyhow? I've asked you about that before. I wonder if anybody knows how to figure that. Let me know if you know.

So, after all, we're all on the same path. After life, comes death—with or without a mirror to remind one of time's passing. In ancient times, men developed religion to deal with maintenance of the social order, to create a moral compass for society and to ponder the questions of life and death. With the promise of everlasting life in some world religions, one wouldn't have to wrestle with this dilemma of being born and then dying. Although looking in the mirror reflects life, it reminds me of Auntie Bum—of death. Too short is the journey we are on—here and now. It is really all about here and now. Do you agree?

In the past dozen years, I've lost many friends and family members. Everybody does. This is nothing about what's new in the world. Rather, as I myself get closer to the end, it's about my awakening to the fact that there is an end. Of course, we always know that. Yet, we don't always realize what that entails. I'm watching how some of my friends deal with monumental losses in their lives.

Mom lived to be almost 98. By anybody's standards, that's a long life, and her death was no surprise. I think I've dealt as well with her leaving us as can be expected—she was a part of my life and I hers for decades. I had a mom longer than most people have their mothers. I have learned that death doesn't kill love. I think about Dad and her every day.

My brother Doug died suddenly, without warning. I didn't deal so well with that. I say goodbye to him every night before going to sleep. He's the only one I tell goodbye.

A friend of mine goes to the gravesite today of her best friend on what would have been his birthday to play some of his favorite tunes.

FROM OREOS TO OLIOS

When he realized he was dying, he had asked her to do this, and she agreed. I can easily picture her standing there alone in the cemetery playing her fiddle. She loved him. He was her family's best friend for over 20 years. He watched her children grow up. If there is a heaven, I think he would have been looking down and smiling at her.

Another friend was a pioneer in the kidney transplant scene at Johns Hopkins. Her husband needed a kidney, and although she wanted to give him hers, it wasn't compatible. Instead, she donated her kidney to someone who needed it, and someone whose kidney was compatible to her husband's donated to him. Thus began multiple-way kidney transplants. Their pioneering has mushroomed into 'dozen-way' transplants.

Her husband died several years later, but his replacement kidney functioned until his death from other causes. This couple had a long and extraordinary life together.

Two honored guests at her husband's memorial were the other donor and the recipient of her kidney in this multiple transplant. Life and love go on in ways unseen.

Another friend has spent the past several months taking care of her partner and husband of the past 49 years. Breaking a hip is often the beginning of the end. Her mate broke his and spent a few months in a local rehabilitation nursing home. Members of their church built a ramp into their house so he could be wheeled in to spend Thanksgiving Day with the whole family. He never returned to the nursing home.

Instead, he stayed at home where he wanted to be with his wife taking care of him until the end. She had many sleepless nights. I know she was exhausted. She did what many spouses couldn't do— she took care of his every need so he could live out the rest of his days at home from November to March. She has done the extraordinary. Serene doesn't describe her face at his funeral. Her strong religious beliefs carried her through both the long illness and his death. Yes, she still cries when alone.

Human beings are the only species who love and know at the same time that there will be an end. Death happens. But, so does love. And, it never dies.

Now, write your stories for those whom you love.

Would you like to see your manuscript become a book?

If you are interested in becoming a PublishAmerica author, please submit your manuscript for possible publication to us at:

acquisitions@publishamerica.com

You may also mail in your manuscript to:

**PublishAmerica
PO Box 151
Frederick, MD 21705**

www.publishamerica.com

CPSIA information can be obtained at www.ICGtesting.com
260170BV00001B/119/P